SEARCHING
— FOR —
MYSELF

SEARCHING FOR MYSELF

Emma Condurache

BALBOA.
PRESS
A DIVISION OF HAY HOUSE

Copyright © 2012 by Emma Condurache.

All rights reserved. No part of this book may be used or reproduced by any means, graphic, electronic, or mechanical, including photocopying, recording, taping or by any information storage retrieval system without the written permission of the publisher except in the case of brief quotations embodied in critical articles and reviews.

ISBN: 978-1-4525-5041-1 (sc)
ISBN: 978-1-4525-5042-8 (e)
ISBN: 978-1-4525-5043-5 (hc)

Library of Congress Control Number: 2012906427

Balboa Press books may be ordered through booksellers or by contacting:

Balboa Press
A Division of Hay House
1663 Liberty Drive
Bloomington, IN 47403
www.balboapress.com
1-(877) 407-4847

Because of the dynamic nature of the Internet, any web addresses or links contained in this book may have changed since publication and may no longer be valid. The views expressed in this work are solely those of the author and do not necessarily reflect the views of the publisher, and the publisher hereby disclaims any responsibility for them.

The author of this book does not dispense medical advice or prescribe the use of any technique as a form of treatment for physical, emotional, or medical problems without the advice of a physician, either directly or indirectly. The intent of the author is only to offer information of a general nature to help you in your quest for emotional and spiritual well-being. In the event you use any of the information in this book for yourself, which is your constitutional right, the author and the publisher assume no responsibility for your actions.

Any people depicted in stock imagery provided by Thinkstock are models, and such images are being used for illustrative purposes only.

Certain stock imagery © Thinkstock.

Printed in the United States of America

Balboa Press rev. date: 06/12/12

I am Ema O'Neill, a totally untypical name for a Romanian. I am 35, not married and no kids. I had never been sure I was ready to engage in a marriage relationship with the whole package: husband, children and in-laws. Something was missing but at that time I was not able to put my finger on a certain issue.

I was born in Romania before 1989, the year of the Revolution, as many call it. I have never met my mother; I have been told she died when I was born and this put a lot of serious questions and raised question marks on my existence. I often wondered *"why me?"* is alive and which is the lesson I should learn from this. Who was my mother and how she looked like were questions I fell asleep with and tears wetting my pillow. I was, in a way or another, looking for her in every older woman I met along the way: my nannies, my teachers, the women from my family and the ones I met along the way. None of them gave me a satisfactory image of a motherly figure. I unconsciously loved her and wanted, for many times, to turn back time and be again at the stage I was inside her and most probably happy. I wanted to be unborn and stay inside her forever.

I tried to understand why I was not willing to build a home of my own and I started to investigate the idea of not living the same "story" my mother lived. I was scared to meet a man and fall in love with and have a child and die at our baby's birth.

So I occupied all my time with ... work. I looked for and got a dynamic job and kept learning and growing in a career till I got to the point of understanding that ... this was not enough. All my life was concentrated around work but this was not enough to make me feel complete. That was the moment I started to seriously question my present and my past. When putting together all the information about my roots, I was surprised to find out how little I knew. The only ancestors I knew were coming from my father's side: my father's parents. Nothing about my mothers'. I was told my mother died at my birth, but what about my mothers' parents? "She grew up in an orphanage", my father used to tell me until I was 14. However I started to get suspicious when the subject was always changed when talking about my mother. "You will understand later", was the answer typical received when asking about her. After a while I stopped asking ...

When Revolution started I was already 14 and getting ready for the winter holidays. I still remember I was baking cookies with two of my cousins. I was so scared about the idea of change to such an extent that I forgot the cookies in the oven till they got burnt. I still remember that I felt like in a dream and had no idea if I could do something about it or not. The images on TV were so shocking and continuously interrupted that I gave up watching. My cousins were loudly crying about the "terrorists" coming, even though none of us really knew the meaning of this word. I had no idea if my father was safe and sound (he was at work) or if I would ever see him again.

Only thinking about losing him too made me freeze. I felt like I was alone in the world: me, a lost child, with no one around (my father's parents were not living in the same city with us) and the rest of the world. I realized then that you never have total control on your life and all the literature I read was just ... literature. My nightmare was short-lived and seemed to finish once my father got home that day. Somehow that was only the beginning of my real life because it seemed that all I have lived till that moment was nothing but a lie.

I spent the last days of 1989 packing the most important things of my life: the book "Le petit prince", the only thing left from my mother; her handwriting was nearly seen on the first page as my touch on that page was the only physical connection with her; some postcards from my holidays, a couple of black and white photos with my colleagues, teachers and my best two friends, the pioneers' scarf with all my colleagues' signature on it. My first 14 years of life had to "fit in" a small suitcase. We were supposed to leave for the States in less than 48 hours. I did not understand why all this rush and especially the fact that I was asked not to mention anything to any of my friends. Those days were the last ones when I saw my grandfather. Since my grandmother had passed away two years before, he was the only one I could say goodbye to. He seemed to know exactly what was going on as he burst into tears when we said "Good bye". I always thought he knew much more than I was told and expected not to see me again! He was right; he passed away six months later. The "goodbye" image was the last souvenir from him I carry with me.

In my first hours after I left behind the "iron curtain", I was looking at the people I was meeting in my new life: passengers from different flights waiting to board, people at the customs, people waiting in the airports' waiting halls, people behind the windows waiving "good byes". They seemed so different than I expected. Some seemed sad, some tired, some angry, some indifferent, some happy, some anxious. I was expecting to see only smiley faces on the other side of "the curtain" but they seemed to be as "normal" as we were. We were so limited in our choices as the regime imposed a limitation on the information available but also by the limitation of information we had; all these people I was looking at had something very precious we did not had before 1989: the freedom. I was completely surprised to find that all this freedom was not visible imprinted on their faces as I was expected. They seemed as "normal" as we looked like. I was wondering though what their story was, if they had dreams and plans. I was trying to think about my life and could not figure out how it was going to be. I knew that my life was turning on a different direction but I had no idea in which way. The freedom of moving was the only clear thing for me at that point. Knowing that I will be able to travel from a part of the world to the other, gave me new hopes and wings. What I found frustrating was that, at this point, I could not say a word in creating my own life. The decision for the new direction was taken by my father and I had not even been asked about it. He was writing my life and I had no input to it. Just like a pilot that does not ask if you agree to take left, right or just go straight ahead when you are in his plane. I promised myself to take all the strings of my life in my own hands as soon as I could. I was 14 then and so, I had to wait until I was 21 if American law was applied in my case.

After more than 24 hours "in the air" and our transfer stop in Paris, the very first days of 1990 found both me and my father in the States. We finally arrived at our new house. I still remember my head felt like burning. I was told to ask no questions so that the first day was a real nightmare to me. The silence felt so heavy that I was gladly ready to change it with any painful fight. My father's eyes were darker and darker and just looking at him made me more and more weary. I felt all the tension around like a powerful cloud landing on my head and I knew that this trip and those moments would totally change my life. I had no idea how much. I had a past of 14 years in an ex-communist country, and now I had to face a new world. Overnight I got the new name, a new passport, a new life. No grandparents, no friends and no idea where I was heading to. Talking to my father in those moments seemed to be the worst case scenario.

A person my father seemed to know expected us at the airport and helped with the two small pieces of baggage we had.

"Is this all your baggage?" he asked in a tone of surprise.

"All our lives are in these small suitcases", my father replied. I found it, even then, at 14, a very sad reply. I promised myself to be "richer" when I would be my father's age. I had no idea, at that point, that more is not always better. It is a known fact that a light luggage can save your life in many circumstances. Caring your past through your life can seriously hurt not only your hands but also your health. Leaving the past behind but keeping the lessons makes it easier to fly.

"I supposed you are both tired, let me show your new home", the strange man replied.

After two days of sleeping, I started coming back to life. We were accommodated in a nice small house and a new life was supposed to be included in the package. The next weeks I tried to adjust to the new city. Huge buildings, huge supermarkets with tens of chocolate and coffee types seemed to be unreal for the 14 years old child raised in the other part of the world. I pinched myself more than once to see if I was dreaming or if everything was real. I was looking at all the people just like they were blessed to have so many things and be able to afford them. I had at the same time flashes from the moments I was lighting the candles for the dead teenagers in Universitatii Square back home. I had moments when I was between my past and my present as if they were fighting for sharing the same moment.

"Everything will be all right, you will see. We now start a new life, a better one. You have no idea how blessed we are to be here, at this moment", my father was continuously repeating.

I saw no sense or logic in any of his words but I had no courage to interrupt him. In my last 14 years I learned to keep all my emotions and words mostly to myself. I used to talk to myself and no one else because I was too scared that my wounds will be discovered. I learned to hide them so well that it was hard even for me to rediscover and heal them in the years after.

Now I was on a new continent with no friends and apparently no roots. Luckily I was speaking English pretty well and this helped. It was for the first time I was really grateful for the most difficult English teachers I got in school. I used to carry out whole monologues inside my head in English and they were really useful for a Romanian girl. Now I changed the "old pattern" by talking English out loud and Romanian with my father and myself. Strange is life itself ...

My first months in the States were the most difficult ones. Not because of the quality of life but due to the new environment and especially to my new colleagues. Coming from a place they have recently heard of as the most "horrible" one on Earth, made me cry over on many nights. I learned at that point that no matter how much you can learn at school, there are lessons you learn only by direct experimentation. The "horrible" place was the only one I knew and my only moral support and it represented, till that point, all my life. My friends, my colleagues, the little flower garden I was taking care of and had to leave behind, even the worst teachers and colleagues from "that" life now seemed to be from another life. I felt, in a strange way, that I was abandoned again (first by my own mother, even if she only passed away) and felt that this time not only my mother died but all my life. I felt I was like a ship in a troubled sea and hesitated to go to the future as I was still having doubts on about my present. The past months seemed to have no logic at all and I was desperately trying to find a reason *"why"* I did not understand anything from it. I was walking like a "dead but alive" person, in someone else's dream and life.

I was often waking up in the middle of the night having no idea where I was and what language I should speak but learned to live with it. Romanian words were mixed with English ones. One night I found myself making a plan to find my own roots. I was the main character in my own play and started to make a plan for saving money and hire a private detective. I had no idea how much this decision will weight on the "resources" I had in "my pocket" at that time but I found, for the first time in my life, a clear purpose in my life. And this meant more than focusing on school. I started working on in extra school activities and considerably opening my horizon. I made a list with my "favorite things to do" and that I could get extra money from. I have always felt some curios resonance and "security" when speaking French and this created me the "space" for spending some time in improving this language and then teaching it to others. It was like a language my heart understood and was happy every time it was spoken. I also started writing for the school magazine and I used this opportunity to express my feelings in writing. Not only did this helped with my school essays but also became an effective true therapy for me. Reading these notes after years I realized how "broken" I felt in those moments of my life. I felt a great eagerness to write especially when feelings such as upsets, hurts or abandonment visited me. These notes became closer to me than anything else before. My past seemed to lose the importance it used to have, my friends, my life in Romania, my grandparents, they all became memories from another life.

"Everything will be ok, you will see", my father kept saying to me.

I started wondering if he was talking to me or if he was trying to encourage himself. I guess he knew nothing more than I did at that time, about where life would be taking us. I was always looking at him as the only one knowing precisely all the steps of his life and implicitly mine but, for the first time, I felt that he had no control or idea over our new life. He was also struggling to find his own place in the new life. Besides, having a child to take care of was probably more burdening for him. I understood that and did my best to "compensate" for the situation.

"All you have to do is go to school, learn and you will see that everything will be just fine. All you have to do is give your best at school. All you need to do is try to be the best and you will succeed in everything", he kept saying.

I was getting the best marks and I have to admit that in many areas I knew the lessons before the teacher taught it. The theory topics seemed one year behind from what I studied in Romania so I was just repeating the year. Besides, all I had to do was learn and study and this was my main focus at that time. Being alone was not something new to me and did not bother me too much. I learnt to have "silence" and "patience" as my best friends. I was struggling not to forget pieces from my past; writing letters to my Romanian friends every other week seemed to be the best solution at that time even though I knew I was not part of their universe anymore. As expected, the connection with them lost its grip on me, the ties became weaker and weaker, and sequences images of my past seemed to fade away. In order to survive in my new life, I needed to make some "clearance" room in my memories so that new moments may enter. I still remembered though and laughed just thinking about our video parties, pioneers festivities and playing outside all day long during our holidays. I remembered not having a large variety of sweets but different types of fruits and home made marmalade, I had no idea what a computer was but I had full access to outdoor games. For me, "Nine stones", "Country, country, we want soldiers", "Geese and hunters" were essential games but for my American colleagues they all seemed hard to explain and difficult to understand. In those days, our childhood seem to have no flaw. I remembered how we shared a chocolate not bigger than a child's hand in four or even six pieces and were very happy to have it. Probably sharing it made it taste so good.

I admit that the new world I was suddenly "sent to" was totally differently from the one I was coming from. In Romania we were faced with scarcity, now we were faced with diversity, starting from food and ending with books, magazines, clothes. Also, the school rules seemed more relaxed, the whole system seemed to let you create and not force you to "fit" in the same matrix; this got me scared but at the same time considerably challenged me. I have been taught to "stay in my own square, exactly on my spot" and not attract too much attention. Now I was asked to stand out in a crowd. This reality seemed so full of contradictions and many times I felt like I was in between two different worlds. In fact I was in the middle and had not decided which one was better for me. It felt strange to be on one side and not the other one; by choosing one of them, I had the impression that I would betray the other "reality" and got a little bit confused. Besides, spending much of my time in the library, gave me more information about the country I was coming from. The history I learned at school started to have "leaks". Facts I always took for granted had different data; it was the same with my own life story so that was no surprise I started to identify it with my own history. The fact that I knew so little about my past and roots started to raise more questions than I expected.

Now, when I look back, I realize that my first 30 years were "dedicated" to my father's dreams and "covering" all his requests: be great at school, do not create problems, and keep myself fit. The only thing I did not do was to get married and this was probably due to the fact that he had never insisted too much on the subject. No wonder that, in a very subtle way, my first 30 years I was faithful into fulfilling my "father's list", in order to be loved by him. We all probably do the same thing. We are so afraid that our parents will stop loving us if we do not go with their expectations. But somehow, by "covering" his expectations, I betrayed my own dreams and expectations as it was impossible to follow two different roads at the same time. My first 30 years I did my best to accumulate as much information as I could, not only from books but also from my own experiences of others'. Once I turned 30, I started to select, review and rearrange all the information and get rid of the ones I did not need and vibrate with. Much info already expired so that I found many gaps into my own life and I started to try filling them. I found that perspective over life itself had the biggest leaks but guessed that this was an issue due to totally different background I had experienced. Somehow, I realized that it was pure luck for me as it made me more flexible than I could have expected to become. And this flexibility taught me that things are not the way I want them to be. People are the way they are. Sometimes they are not even aware of the fact that they are "following" a certain pattern the parents have drawn for them. It is an easy way as it does not imply too many risks. You are following the same, beaten path everyone had followed before. And expect to have pretty much the same outcome as they had. The big issue is when you are not getting the results you expected. We are not living in the same environment as they did, let's face it! So, how can we expect to get the same "prizes" as they did? Following your own way is not easy but, at least, it gives you the satisfaction that you followed your own way and not "copied" it from someone else. Besides, the outcomes can be amazingly rewarding. You can find things inside yourself you did not even think about, you can discover things you did not even guess you have hidden inside. Once you want to be an actor, you will do your best to become one even if everyone around wants you to be a doctor only because you are better paid. If you want to be an actor, all your passion will help you carry the entire "luggage" and become a bright one. When I look around I see that most of us living in a moment where we're doing jobs we do not want but were directed to. No wonder we get tired and bored, even though we are paid well enough to afford not to be. The good news is that it is never too late to come back on our own path and follow it. It is never too late to see the divine light inside us and ask it to guide us. It is only a matter of choice and responsibility because, after all, everything is allowed as long as you are taking full responsibility for your choice.

Following your own path is not easy and it is covered with many doubts, fears and disappointments. But, you must remember, we are never alone. Angels are next to us, just waiting to ask for their help. It is that easy since we are used to work hard for all our achievements. Just ask for their help. Once we follow our own paths, they can help by releasing the burden of our thoughts, worries, and doubts. Being happy and healthy, you have more resources available to help the other people, with joy and passion. If your soul is dried, you are able to help neither you nor others.

I remember having long evening monologues with my angels and implicitly with my mother. I wanted to make my life worth it for both of us. I was hoping she was proud of me and watched over me from Heaven. I was asking all my angels to protect me, my father, my friends and all my non-friends for making me better. The short prayer my grandmother taught me was accompanying me each night and that made me feel stronger in a non understandable way.

"Angel of God, you are my guardian
Spread your light over me tonight.
Lead me, guard me and advise me.

> *I have been given to you through*
> *The mercy and care of God.*
> *Angel, my little angel,*
> *Pray to God for my little soul*
> *And wherever I am, be around me.*
> *From today till night until I die.*
> *I am small, you make me big*
> *I am weak, you make me strong.*
> *And be with me everywhere*
> *And keep me away from all bad things*
> *And take good care of me."*

For many nights I imagined I was in the arms of an angel that took care of me. I felt safe, protected and warm. And even though tears were always running on my face, I felt comforted and warm. I used this image so often that it became my "bed time story". I do not even remember when I started doing that, it seemed that it was always there and just waiting for me to remember it. It helped me during all my life. And in all the moments I felt there was too much anger or sadness, I talked to my angels and put all these emotions into their hands. I knew they know better how to deal with them. I have always felt a huge relief once I let myself do that.

I had felt, in a strange way and for many years, I was paying a price it was not even mine; only thinking about it made me ashamed. Besides, for too many times I had the strange feeling that once I was sure I closed a chapter and was ready to enjoy the results I only found out that there are other and other bridges I have to build and then pass cross; that made me not only angry but really disappointed. When thinking I thought was at the end of the journey, I got new info and needed to start all over again and again without even knowing the results of the previous journey. Not even I wouldn't even get some rest after the previous journey when I was being forced to start a new one. Looking at the entire situation now, I realize that the most annoying thing was that I was not even asked if I agree with it or not. I might have agreed up there with the entire "plan" (if it is real what is said that we choose the things we want to experience once we are here, on earth) but since I did not remember a word, I had to follow it and this made me really angry. But I guess the soul knows well all the steps and only the mind is asking for "approvals" and "recognition" so that it is not kept outside the decision process. The minute I thought I was finally closer to what I wanted most in this life, I was confronted with details from my past or present so that it seemed that instead of having a glass of wine for celebrating the success I had the same glass of wine but to let my tears get out. In those moments I saw no sense and direction but this process made me more conscious that life is more than what we see at a first glance and I had to admit that the more I looked into it, the less I understood. Maybe there is no logic in all that is happening. The more logic you are looking for, the less you find. So, I practice the same process over and over again: accept that I can not swim against the wave. And then relax and let myself go with the flow. This is the best I can do. Put all my force in staying alive and not get drowned.

Since my plan of traveling and discovering my roots involved serious financial resources, I knew I needed to become financially independent as soon as possible. Traveling was the most powerful discovered tool for keeping myself together so with all my qualifications I looked for a job that included traveling as a request.

I celebrated my 25th anniversary in France. It was a wonder to see that the connection I have always felt with this land was real. I had had no idea at that time that the moment to "search for myself" would start exactly at that point. After ten days spent in France, I came back to the States and decided to use a significant part of my savings for traveling to this country. At that moment, it was just like the only point of interest on my internal map. I still remember that on my first night in this country I had a very interesting dream.

I was driving in winter and trying to find some green color in the whole landscape as everything was white: the road, the sky, the mountains. At some point, after many miles of the same picture covered in white, I noticed a small drop of grass that became bigger and bigger, a good sign for me that I was closer and closer. I got off the car and started walking on the grass; every single step I took left a bunch of flowers behind my steps, coming out of nowhere; this encouraged me to jump just like a child not only to assure myself they were coming out of my feet but also to get more and more flowers. It was one of the happiest moments of my life. It was even more unbelievable as we were in June so there was no logical connection with winter.

I knew then, as I do today, that there are many unexplainable but wonderful connections between things. And once you believe in them, you know that miracles do happen.

My next years were divided mainly between my work and actual traveling. In ten years I had already seen most of Europe, parts of Asia and most part of America. As for France, I had already been there seven times in the last ten years. My inner soul was shouting to come back, again and again to this place.

When I turned 30, my father got married with a nice Romanian woman, "brutally disintegrated" from the same country we were coming from. As a very much appreciated musician, she left for a concert to the States and decided not to come back and requested political asylum. Her meeting with my father made him more receptive to the world. I somehow understood that they were both a support for each other since they both shared common experiences in the relation to their mother country. It was the first time I heard my father laughing and the first time when I cried just thinking about it. It was the first time I understood what being born "at the right place and the right time" meant. Seeing my father married with Maria, gave me the courage to rent my own apartment, closer to the University and my working place. This gave me more space and time for myself. All the financial support from my father was considered, by me, additional income for my traveling plans. We were sharing the weekends and holidays inside the family.

I secretly intended to move to France one day; till then the plan was to do my best to get a job that would allow me to travel more to this country. Finding this country so confusingly fascinating, made me realize that my life, my roots, my past were still very unclear to me; I remembered that at some point in my past I promised myself to find out more about my roots. For different reasons, the plan was "on hold" and focused more on traveling than finding all the pieces from that puzzle.

On my 34 anniversary I tried to approach the "roots" subject with my father but did not find enough courage to finalize it. Then, one day, in spring, when joining my father and his wife for the weekend, I decided to have one more try on the same subject. All my secret research was blocked and I hoped that my father could give a hand. I did not want to make him remember all the painful moments but I needed to know the truth. I realized that I was scared of finding out new things I did not want to know about his past and implicitly mine I was postponing the moment for as long as I could. Knowing nothing about it, did not hurt as much as it might had if I found out things I did not like. However, the stakes of not knowing became too high so that I was determined to have it all revealed. I felt that as long as I was not able to know my roots, I would never be able to live in peace, so it became an obsessive thought I needed to clear out.

"I know I have never seemed to be too curios in finding more about my past but there are things I need to know. I have always behaved and asked nothing so that you do not feel bad about it. But, dad, it is time for me to know. I am more than 30, and I do not feel the urge to have my own family and this worries me a little bit. I traveled half the world but did not succeed to find myself. I was thinking that if I get to know my past, I have more chances to understand my present and build my future. There are things I need to know. I think I deserve that. I need to know about my roots and what really happened in my past."

Even though I prepared myself for this moment years before, I felt a strong grip in my throat after the last sentence. I was praying for all my angels' help. They were the only ones I had had with me all the time and I was counting on their help. I read somewhere that once you know your past and take it the way it is, in the meaning of integrating it as part of your life, your life gets more simple. In my case, there were many pieces missing from my life's puzzle. I did not expect only beautiful things, but at least finding them and giving them a place in my heart, were expected to ease the situation.

"What do you want to know?" my father calmly replied.

"All you can tell me", I quickly said. "Starting with my birth would be very good."

"Well, it will take some time", he replied.

"I waited all my life for these answers, dad. I think I trained my patience pretty well". I was surprised to hear my voice sound so confident. I knew the angels were all around this situation, giving me courage and love.

"Dad, I find it very confusing not to be able to find my own place. I seem to belong nowhere. I am born in one part of the world, I am extremely and strangely attracted by another place on the planet while I live in another part. This is not only confusing but frustrating. And I ask myself why I am not able to have a family of my own. I do not know where I came from, dad, and it is extremely difficult to try to build something on a sandy place. I seem not to "fit" anywhere. No mater what you built on sand, it will not last, it is not working. I am spinning round and round and I am really tired. I want to do something good with my life but I cannot see the road I am going on. I do not know who I am, what my roots are, seems like the past I know is more and more unclear. Please help me! I need your help! I know this might bring you painful memories, but you are the only one who can help", I said in one breath.

"I was always afraid of this moment", dad said "but it is a relief you are asking. There are so many things I kept for myself hoping that this way I can protect you but I realize that you are stronger than I have ever imagined and hoped for. I am aware that I could not "cover" the mother role for you and not even tried to and I hope that once I give you all the details, you are not going to hate me".

"How can I hate you, dad? I know that nothing has been easier for you, too. Maybe this is the first adult conversation we have ever had. And maybe giving me all the answers I need, we can both heal our own wounds".

"How was my mother, dad? How come I have never seen any picture of her in our house? When I pray at night I do not even know how she looks like and try to imagine her face but every time it seems to change. When I was a kid, I used to"borrow" familiar faces and pray to them. I remember that, at some point, I was identifying my mother's face so much with my teacher of Romanian that the second day I saw her at school I was almost shocked and so ashamed, at the same time. I had a very serious moment of confusion when thinking she was my mother. And I was so ashamed for that! Since then I loved and hated this teacher for that, even though she had no blame for this" I ended in a soft voice just like speaking to myself.

"You look so much like your mother! Same beautiful face, same smile, even the same style of dressing up, even if you have never met her! She was the most beautiful women I have ever seen! When I see you, I see her and every moment I look at you is a moment of happiness and pain. You have the same way of talking and walking and the same sophisticated intelligence she had. After your birth, I could not bear to see her only in pictures so that I threw away all the photos she was in. It was too much for me. You have to promise me you are not going to hate me after I tell you this …"

"How can I hate you, dad? You are the only person, even if almost catatonic I had by my side all these years. How can I hate you? Tell me about my mother, please. How did you meet?" I quickly added.

I had never imagined you can miss someone you have never met. And God, did I miss her! Talking about her, even after so many years, made me feel closer to her!

"I was invited by one of my best friends, to a reception at the French Embassy. She was the most beautiful woman I have ever seen. I still remember my heart beating like crazy when I asked her for a dance. I could not believe my heart can endure so much happiness. When I felt her in my arms, I knew she was the one I was always looking for. I felt so blessed she was granting me that dance. I could never expect she would accept it. She was like an angel coming straight from Heaven. We both completely felt in love. I can still remember the feeling, even though it's been more than 35 years since that moment. I guess these moments you can never forget ..."

I was all in tears. Finally, my life was getting shape. I felt so blessed and grateful to know that I was born out of a love story.

"It is not a coincidence you are so attracted to France and I knew the first time you told me you want to go there that you will find certain ties with this land. Your mother was born in France and came to Romania for a conference. It is at that reception that we met and fell in love. Unfortunately the price we had to pay for this love was too high. And I am afraid that you are paying part of it, too. I am so sorry, my angel! All I want is for you to be happy! For all our pain not to be in vain, I want you to have a happy life! I know you have already paid enough! All I want is for you to be happy!" he added in tears.

I have never seen him crying before and that scared me. All the difficult times we went through together, he knew how to hide his own pain and now he was crying.

"What are you trying to say, dad? You are really scaring me now, you know? Please do not cry. What do you mean? What happened? What do you mean I paid the price for that? I do not get it."

"Our love story was not "approved" by the "Party" from those days. We were making plans for our future. We planed to stay in Romania, have you and grow old together as a family. After you were born, your mother was sent to France and I was "discredited" from work for "getting involved with the foreigners". She could not even see you after your birth, it was decided that you, as a Romanian citizen, stay with me, in Romania, and she was sent back to France. I have never heard anything from her ever since even though I was trying to get in touch with her …"

My head was all spinning. I felt like sea sick and altitude sick all at the same time. I felt my brain refusing to process any information, my soul was confused, and my heart broken.

"Wait a minute, you mean, my mother might be still alive? Is it what you are trying to tell me? She might be alive and live in France? So, every single time I felt the impulse to go there I was, in an unconscious was, trying to meet my mother? Just like a "blood cry"?"

I felt not only sick but also strangely weak and strong at the same time. All my past seemed to overwhelm me and I had the impression it would soon suffocate me. The words I once read somewhere "what does not kill you makes you stronger" seemed meaningless in those moments and made no sense. I felt the pain of every single word, in every molecule of my body. I started crying like a fountain cries when turned on but realized it only when my nose could not face anymore. Fragments of all my "cursed" life seemed to come back to life over and over again with no real logic or sense. In fact, nothing seemed to make any sense in those moments. I wanted to wake up but felt my knees would not be able to carry the heaviness of my head. I felt I was in a labyrinth and at the same time in a tomb. Fortunately Maria came in and probably realized what kind of heavy grey clouds were floating around us. I looked at my father and I saw a disfigured face. I was feeling so much sympathy but also so many mixed feelings at that moment. I had no idea how my father could hide such a painful secret for so many years. The love of his life, my mother, might be there somewhere and he hides it from me for so many years. I was able to understand, as long as I was in Romania, it was probably "safe" to keep it away from me, but since we came here, to the US, how could he have kept this secret? I imagined my mother as an angel watching me every single night and now I find out that she might be alive. My head was like a huge piece if iron torturing my whole body.

"Drink this tea. It will make you feel better. Some sleep will also help. Tomorrow is another day. Everything looks better when the sun is up."

I heard Maria just like in a dream. I went to my room and collapsed in bed. At some point, I fell asleep.

I wake up with a strange feeling as if I drank too much alcohol. For a second I thought that the previous day would be only a dream but when I saw my eyes in the mirror I knew it was not. I could not face my father and was praying not to see him for a while. I remembered him telling he hopes I wouldn't hate him and now I was finally getting the meaning of his words. My stomach felt highly contracted. I went outside under the tree I was always coming to talk to ever since my first day in our new house. He knew all my secrets. I was afraid that the new secret was too much even for him. I was afraid but at the same time hoped that the whole sky would go down on me and make me disappear at once. I did not want to die but was not too keen on living either. I was looking at the clouds and asked for my angels' help. I was begging for a sign of encouragement. I was, for the first time, finding some logic in my impossibility to have my own family and many things seemed to get shape and make sense. Might have fallen asleep because the moment I opened my eyes the sun was already going down and Maria was next to me.

"Hi".

"Hi".

"I can not pretend I know what you feel but if there is anything I can do to help, I am here. I know I am not your mother and I have never pretended or tried to be but if there is anything I can do, please let me know. I just wanted to let you know I am here."

I was incapable of saying anything, but I knew tears were running down on my face when I felt Maria's hand on my cheeks. She was one of the kindest persons I have ever met. I did not remember having a conversation longer than ten minutes in all our life as a family but I knew there were many moments when we understood each other just looking in each other's eyes. Words were too much then and it was the same now.

"Some wounds seem too deep and impossible to be cured but they eventually will, I promise you," she added.

"Help me find my mother, please", I suddenly said and put my head on her arms. "Please, help me find her", I continued.

"I promise I will. This is a promise", she finally said into tears. "Let's go in and have something to eat. You have had nothing all day long. We can start working on a plan for finding her, too. Come on, let's get in. It is getting cold."

I felt, in that second, I found a new reason for going on. Getting to meet my mother was an impossible dream to me up to now and suddenly in only a couple of hours my life was all upside down. This type of event was something I was afraid of all my life. On the other hand, just the thought that I might meet my mother made me realize that all the effort was worth it.

The next two weeks I was in between my work and talking to Maria. She contacted her friends and relatives from Romania, signed Requests Forms for getting more information about my mother and even hired a private detective. I knew she was working closely with my father but I was not prepared to see him yet. I did not hate him but I was afraid to look in his eyes. I was too afraid how I would react to his look and have no control over it. Or the words I could have said to him. I knew the moment I needed to face him would come eventually but hoped it would be delayed as much as possible. I was working additional hours as a new client was acquired and needed extra hours for different projects. Not only did that keep my mind busy over other things but in the evenings I felt so tired that I would instantly fall asleep. I was saving all the money I could get. I was planning to go to France in the beginning of June and there were only two months left. I had no idea which point from France I would start my search from but I was praying for my angels' help. I knew that at the right time, I will get the right piece of information. I was in a stage of mixed feelings directed not personally to my father but to the entire situation: betrayal, anger and upset, happiness that maybe I could find my mother, scared of what might come out of this and of meeting her.

I have always considered my mother a dream I wished for. Even though I knew I would never meet her, somehow, in my deepest secret dreams, I imagined I had conversations with her and I was guided by her. Now, realizing that this dream might come true gave me more fear than anything else. In my mind, she was perfect, placed on a pedestal while I was just like any other mortal praying to her. I was aware that the new situation I was facing might destroy this image, just by making it real.

If it is true what they say that we decide our own destiny and write our own life before we get here, on Earth, I was wondering why I had chosen this "strange" role to play. And then I would imagine that from out there, from the sky or the place we look down from, all things seem much easier than from here. We are all coming perfectly "equipped" with everything we need and then everything seems so very complicated as we forget why we came here for and are confused and scared and angry. Life is supposed to be easy. However, all we do ever since we get here is sabotage our own lives. And this is probably because we are so afraid of the power we have within us. If we still remember who we are and what our mission is, then we would be most probably terrified of that power. "Luckily", there is always someone or something that makes us believe we can not do all we dream of. However if we do not believe in our power and dreams, no one else does. We are all writing our own story. We are the only ones who know our dreams and have the power to accomplish them. We all have the ability to make a change and a difference in our own present and history.

I had no idea how I came to this point in my life and what I should learn from it (and maybe I will not know until I go up there, at "home") but since I chose to be here, at this point with other human beings, I should do my best to enjoy what's left of my time here the best I could. Even though I am not able to smile and be happy all the time, the moments I am happy are more abundant than the sad ones so when I look back at my life and all the moments gathered under the name of "my life" I would be able to enjoy them again only by knowing that I lived my life and not another's.

I was often talking to myself in silence as I knew that strength pays visits when talking in silence. I realized that I received the best answers in silence most probably due to the fact that intuition comes in silence. If you can make silence your ally, you discover the way to the real you. The "bridge" between you and "your core" gives you access to the divine part we are all connected to when sleeping but rarely access it in our "daily life"; and by not accessing it day and night, we forget about this access to our inner us. In a strange way, we do refuse our right to our full self.

We are usually looking for things in other places instead of looking for them inside ourselves. Once we are looking for love in another person, we expect that person to cover our needs of love and unconsciously put a burden on his/ her shoulders. Once we look and find love inside ourselves, it is so sufficient that all the excess we find in the other person makes us even more happy and loved. I do not believe in "too much love will kill you" as we never have too much love. I mean love not "sick love" or possessive love but pure love, the one that heals and fulfills.

I knew I was not able to understand myself by asking the others to do that. I completely understood how selfish I was during my life. Asking for the people around you to understand you when you are not able to understand yourself, is a gesture of complete ignorance and selfishness. Not only that you ask, in the name of love, to be understood but you also place a huge burden on the other people's shoulders. Or is it the fact that we have no idea what love is and we know not how to love ourselves? Are we following the old patters we inherited and think that they can be applied during all times and especially in these times of complete changes?

I tend to agree that the world would be easier if love were our best friend. Faith would also join. If we have faith in love, we have faith in our inner power. If we have faith and speak our truth with love, then our life would be easier.

I love because I love. I have no specific and clear reason for loving. I have always found it confusing when asked "Why do you love me?" and always found myself unprepared for the "right" answer. I love you because I do. Is it a good enough reason? I do not need you to love me so that I love you in return. I just do. Oh, yes, of course, in case you love me too, this is great but it's not the groundwork for me loving you. If I have to find reasons "*why*", I am lost. I love you because you are. No need for more. Maybe we should start loving ourselves more and not be surprised if someone else loves us back for any particular reason. After all, if you consider that we are all interconnected and part of each other, it is not so uncommon to love you for a special reason because loving you is, in a way, loving me.

Love within us helps by giving the support we need all the way. Real love and not the "dependent, addicted" one will make our wings spread, chase all the fears away and connect us to our core, our divine Self. That's why it helps us fly and become free.

True, love starts with yourself as even the Bible say "love your neighbor as much as you love yourself". But if I do not love myself, how can I know what love is and give it to the others, too? And what does love mean for every single person?

Is it respect? Is it pampering, listening, indulging, and taking care? I understand why so many people looked for an answer and did not get it entirely. You can, of course, find the "perfect" answer in books, but the way it applies and resonates with you makes it a personal experience. Life is more complex than I ever thought and I wonder if the people I met in my life had the same questions and if they found their own answers. I was told that "escaping" to relationships or marriages might be a solution but I was wondering if this was the real solution for me. I tried to find my own answer even if it took more time than expected. Might be easier in two as you bring two different life backgrounds and experiences but you need extra communication skills so that you do not create more issues than if you are alone. We all "carry" different "luggage" in relationships and when we lack the maturity to choose its "strong points", we fail. Once we make the inventory of our "luggage" and make our new one by deciding what we can keep or not from our old one, we can start growing a beautiful, mature relation. If we fail in doing this, the base we start building on is going to fall collapse sooner or later. I was wondering if men have the same questions as women do. Then I thought that they might be differently focused but probably face more pressure because women expect them to change and become the persons we want them to be. Even though they do not agree and do not change. It is really unfair what we are doing to each other: we want them to change, they don't. They want us not to change but we do. And if we do not understand this simple fact and fail to communicate we get to feel lonely into our relationships.

I realized that I spent almost all the past weekends under the tree in my father's backyard. The old questions seemed to surface and distract me from the present moment.

Now, looking at my past it did not appear to be, as my mature mind would say, a perfect one. But, accept it or not, this was my past and I had not the power to change it. I then realized it was quite a relief I could not change it as this implies huge responsibility on my shoulder and a burden not only on my destiny but also on the ones involved in the process. As far as I could remember, my life seen through my eyes, as a child, was perfect! Strangely when we grow up, we discover flaws in our past. And the more you look into your past, more mistakes can be found. But after all, my past was part of me, whether I wanted it or not. Denying it, not only brings me unhappiness but also ruins what has been built before. By admitting the facts that took place in my past, it does not implicitly mean accepting it, but just admitting that this is the way things happened. And promise yourself that next time, with all the information coming out of your experience, you would do a better job.

If we put our mind at rest from time to time is just like we put our money into a safe deposit. Not only we know exactly how much we have, but we know we have access to it whenever we need it. If we put love at rest, we feel empty as we find no sense of purpose to go on and moving with the wind. And life with no love is joyless, no inspiration, a burden, restlessness, no appetite for anything. If we put love at rest or in a "safe deposit", we might forget the password and waste it. Love is growing by sharing it and once we are in the flux of love, we are connecting it to our inner us and others' and it gets bigger and bigger.

For the first time in the last weeks, I burst into laugher. I found it all so hilarious. The whole situation: me, my past, my childhood, my worries; all the years I was focused only on making my father proud of me. It seemed like all the moments of my life were so seriously "busy" and could not "afford" any moment of laughter and now I was just "recovering" all the "lost" moments of a good laugh. If everything is just in the moment and the past went, my whole life seemed like a joke, and this was the perfect moment to have a good laugh. I was laughing and bursting into tears at the same time. I just realized how rigid my first 34 years had been and felt sorry for myself. It was like an alarm clock announcing some specific moment and I felt, probably for the first time in my life, grateful for my life. Rigid, tortured, serious, troubled, strange, however defined in my own terms, my life was mine and I was gathering piece by piece into place like in a puzzle. I was looking with astonishment at them and happily crying for this special moment. At that point, I totally and differently understood the expression "getting mad". I had no idea if I was getting stronger or destroyed by the whole situation, but I felt, for the first time in weeks that I was free and able to receive all the support I needed.

I went into the house. My father, at the lamp's light, was reading the newspaper; Maria was just finishing arranging dinner. The last couple of weeks were not easy for any of us.

"Good evening, Maria. Good evening, dad. How are you this beautiful evening?"

They both looked in astonishment to each other and probably considered I went crazy.

"I realized how lucky I am and I need to thank you both for that. I have been quite distracted lately but I am on my path again, so I need to thank you. I know I have never said it before but I love you, dad. And I love you Maria and thank you both for being part of my life. See you tomorrow."

No one said anything. As I was getting to the door of my room, I have heard Maria.

"Aren't you joining us for dinner?"

"No, thank you, I have already had some, thank you. See you tomorrow. Love you."

I had no dinner but I was not hungry. When I entered my room, things seemed so different. The moonlight covered all the things in my room like a smile. I remembered how we perceive things when we go through different moods. I looked at all the things in my room and told them I loved them. I felt so much love inside that seemed to flood all the room. I thanked my angels again. I felt they were there, with me and I was so grateful for that. I felt I have just received a love letter from God. And yes, I felt grateful for that. I felt like my mother was watching over me from somewhere in France and I prayed to meet her when the moment is right for me and for her. And I felt, for the first time, that me, meeting with her, was closer than I might have ever thought. Once I put my head on my pillow I instantly fell asleep.

I woke up when the sun was invading my room. I remembered the feeling: I felt so refreshed. When I got into the living room, I found Maria and my father in the same places I left them the night before.

"Good morning, Maria. Good morning, dad. How are you this beautiful morning? Did you get any sleep? You seem you did not even leave the room …"

"Good morning, sunshine. Coffee?"

"Yes, please. I would love a cup of coffee".

"I hope you are not angry but I was checking on you last night. I was afraid …" started Maria.

" … to be under drugs?"

"I wanted to be sure you were ok." Maria replied. My father was looking at both of us in silence.

"This is funny, you know." I replied. "I thought so too, but given the fact that I didn't have any drugs, I expect you were shocked when I told that I love you. Isn't that right? Is this the only reason why you thought I was under drugs?"

"Well, you never told me this", my father finally articulated.

"I have never said it because I have never heard it from anyone before, dad. I do not complain, but once you do not hear it, you do not know it. I know you have probably been traumatized with all the events in your life. A love you have never been allowed to fulfill, a child coming too soon, a regime that tried to destroy ... I don't know, dad, I suppose it is not easy to face it, no matter how young or old you are. You probably felt the need to hide it to protect yourself from getting crazy that you forget to say it even to your only daughter."

Tears of resentment, happiness and finally relief were coming out from my father's eyes. I have to admit I have never seen my father crying since "the night call" as I used to call it.

"I finally feel I am free. All these years I felt I was in a prison I was afraid to get out. Once I could run from Romania, I did it. I through that was the prison I was in, but the real prison was inside me. And the fences seemed so high I lost the courage to climb them. When you asked me about your mother, I was even more afraid I could lose you too. I tried so much to protect you and had no idea how you would react to all the news that I felt I was going to lose my mind ..."

"I guess it did not kill us after all", I said and started to laugh. "Dad, I need your help to find my mom. I do need to meet her. I need all the info you can get. For the past weeks I made some research with Maria but we did not get too far. We do need your help, all the connections you still have in Romania and France. In fact, we need all the help we can get."

"Of course I will. After all I owe you that much", he replied.

"Maria, can I count on your help, too? I know this is a strange situation, you, the wife, trying to find your husband's former love …"

"I would love to help, sunshine", Maria replied with a smile.

"I really love you Maria, and I love you, dad."

"I love you too, sunshine", said Maria.

"I love you too, angel. We should say it more often …" he replied in a huge smile.

"It definitely sounds great. I have to admit that …"

"We both agree it definitely does".

"Dad, what is my mom's name? I remember you told me …"

"It's Catherine", "Catherine, not Caterina, as I told you. It seemed more Romanian, I was …"

"Catherine, Catherine, Catherine. Sounds so beautiful! I bet she is a very special person. Just saying the name and makes me feel … so good."

The very next morning I wake up with a very strange feeling. It was just like I was in the world but apart from it. I was somewhere up looking at me. I knew that day will mean more than an ordinary day to me. I prayed to my angels to be with me every step of the way and give me strength in case I needed. And I did. I was so right.

It can be really scary to stop from your routine life, with worries, problems to solve, things to do, places you have to get to. If you stop and put all these issues under question, you might feel lost. You realize that you do not "have to" do a lot of things. On the other side, all these things you occupy your life with, give you a sense of "meaning"; you might consider that your life has a purpose. What if you stop for a moment, question your actions a little bit and realize there are things more important for you to do than the things you are daily doing in order not to have time and think about them? It is scary, I can guarantee you that. But once you realize that you are doing the right things for you and for the others, you get happy. I read somewhere that the only thing we are asked to do (mainly) in this life is to be happy. Are you happy? With your life, with the things you are doing? If not, what are you doing to make a change? The moment I am happy, I know that I can make a change, because the world gets one more smile from me. And one smile attracts another one and so on. It is just a matter of choice. My happiness as much as my health, wealth and all the things that affect me are my entire responsibility. As long as we all assume our own responsibility, the world will be less burdened. As long as we are expecting others to make us happy not only that we put a huge burden on their shoulders under the pretext of love but we are all unhappy. It is not fair to ask the others to guess and fulfill your dreams and expectations. But what we can definitely do is to reach out to our own dreams and expectations.

Once I got to the office, I was informed by the Head of the Human Resources department that the whole department I was running was dissolved. The headquarter decided to coordinate all the departments from one point only, and 50%

of all the company was practically dissolved overnight. I was thinking of all the hopes, joy and time spent between the walls of this company. Then I remembered all the times I wanted to leave the company over the last years. I felt many times that I was going into a direction I did not want but had no courage to do it in a different way. I knew I had to stop and get out of that circle but I had no courage to do it. And now, under the circumstances, I was somehow "helped" to do it: go my own way and chose my own direction. I knew I would meet potential difficulties but in the depth of my heart I knew I was going to be fine. It was a little bit strange how many things changed over the last weeks: I had found out I have a mother and now, I have no job.

I had times in my live when I left home just to have a place to come back to. I left for work, even though I did not enjoy it too much but said this was a compromise I need to accept for a while. Now, the "compromise period" was over. I remembered promising myself to have, at some point, the courage to leave it and do something I like and not to be a prisoner of my own habits and my own lifestyle. Having a job made me run away from aspects of my own life, in a way or another. I did not stay too much thinking if this was the road I wanted to go or not. I was often hearing people trying to convince me that this is the situation in life: you do your job, be paid for it, pay your obligations and cover your daily needs. I felt for many times like in a labyrinth tying to get out but eventually getting trapped in the same circle. I remembered that working with children gave me a sense of "normality" I have never experienced before: all things are easier than ever expected. Children see the world from an angle the adults had forgotten in order to survive. They do not know the meaning of many words such as "can not", "allowed", "forbidden". Once you are talking to them, you can realize how much we, as adults, lost on the way. All they have is the present of "today" and take the best out of it. We, the so called "mature adults", are usually stuck in yesterday or tomorrow and are not able to enjoy the only present life offers today.

Once you decide to focus your entire existence on today, things change. I tried it many times and I have to admit you need to practice it many times a day than even considered as we are used to follow the same pattern and a new behavior involves "re-writing" your new laws and rules. Ever since I stopped considering myself a "victim" and my mother's "murderer" and felt blessed for the life she gave me, things started to be different. I was thinking that once I would be able to enjoy most moments of my life for both of us that would make her enjoy my happiness. In this way, I felt I respected and honored her memory and life.

Even though I intended to give up my job, finding myself in this unexpected situation gave me mixed-feelings but I felt, somehow that this was a good present poorly packed however. The management agreed to cover all the last year bonuses and the next three monthly payments. One in one, I would have the necessary amount not only for my trip to France but also a one year out-of-the-market period. The radio was running "the best is still unwritten" song. I started laughing. Only one month ago, I would find this situation impossible to handle, but now I found it even hilarious! This was the reality I was facing with and no logic reason to fight against it. All I could do was to looked at it from a different perspective. Yes, the best is still unwritten. The best is yet to come. I was just praying to have the wisdom to see it.

I was thinking how things started to "match" at this point in my life: I got the chance to stop and review my life, my dreams, and my wishes. Losing my job made me realize that I was stuck in my own life and investigating all of my resources in a direction I neither wanted nor liked. I had to stop and reconsider the whole picture I was in. I am sure there are many people facing the same situation. How everyone is dealing with it, it's really a matter of choice. You can find it convenient to stay in the same situation all your life, even though you hate it, but at least you know how to deal with it so you prefer it to something new; you have no idea how to handle the new situation, even in the long run it is unbelievable better.

It is easy but almost understandable and considered "normal" to hit back when you are hit, to judge whenever you are judged but the real power and courage is not to follow this pattern but to act and react as a human being full of love. If you are paying the same "dues" the others are giving you, not only that you are working with the same, destructive energy but you are as weak as them. When you are "changing" the pattern, you are choosing not to forget the divine part within you, with your own destiny and following your own path. God is everywhere and in all of us but sometimes we forget this and let allow ourselves be "carried" on paths that are not ours.

I intended to go to my rented apartment but I took the road to my dad's house. It was strange to choose the same location as the weekend, but something told me I should go and see him and Maria. My car was stuffed with different things from the office. I did not like carrying them with me but they were personal stuff and represented something to me and no one else. I was so caught up in my own thoughts that I forgot about the packages. I spent all my day in the park across the office where I used to work talking to the sky. Judging from outside, I might have seemed a lost person.

Maria and dad were just having dinner. As they did not expect me to come, they looked surprised but also happy at the same time. It is quite amazing how in all the difficult times we run to our family. I guess you get the real support within your own family. Small or large, with its own secrets, they were my family and I felt blessed for it.

I only said "hi" when dad started to talk.

"I just wanted to call you. We have an extraordinary piece of news." He said very quickly. "Do you remember I told you about my best friend who invited me to that party where I met your mother?"

"Yes, I remember."

"After all these years, I finally got in touch with him and, believe it or not, he has new data about your mother. In fact, this is the most important one after 30 years" he instantly added. "We have an address. She is living in France, as expected, nearby Vernon. So, whenever you are ready, we can go".

I was breathless. I felt part of a game I did not know but had to follow. I was, in only one day, jobless but full of hopes for my personal life. For not giving up on the game, I was offered the prize of more info about my mother. This started to make sense to me. I was a little bit puzzled but ready to discover the "rules" of the new game.

"Dad, with this piece of information, you made my day!"

"But ..." he replied and expected me to continue the sentence.

"But this is something I need to do by myself, if you do not mind. I want to find her by myself. I have no idea what and how I am going to find, do or react when I'll see her, but

I need to do it just by myself. But I promise I will keep you posted every step of the way …"

"Fair enough", he said after a time of reflection.

"Thank you. Besides, I have all the time in the world now. I have just been fired today. Difficult times, they said, cost cutting. I could definitely use this time for myself and finding my mother is the best way to start."

"How in the world …?"

"Really, this is ok. I have never been so convinced about anything. What is she doing for a living? Does she have any children? Is she ok? … I have so many questions …"

"She is considered to be the best French historian writer. And yes, she is living nearby Vernon, in a small cottage. That's all I know. She is supposed to be married but I do not know if she has any children. I have an address though, hopefully correct and you can find out more …"

"Great! I have the information I need to start from. I am just going to take one step at a time; first I'll have a shower!" I ended and started to laugh. "France, I'm coming back. Mom, hope you are ready to meet me" I said in a smile but felt my voice choking.

After all I had no idea what I will find and if I will find her or not. I tried not to rise my expectations too high in this trip and kept telling myself that, even if at the end of this trip, I will not be satisfied with the result, in the sense that I would not meet my mother or she would not accept to see me, at least I tried to reach this dream. Only a couple of months ago, having a mother was an impossible dream and now it was just like a gift offered to me.

I was in an euphoric state of mind and soul and this confused me. I knew that a good bath and rest will do their own work.

I had just finished a day fully charged with emotional mixed felling and I felt an urge to stay outside for a while and talk to my tree and angels. Once I had the "conversation", I felt blessed for all the changes over the last weeks.

I often hear that you need to live in the present and not to worry about your future or past because present is the only thing you have. However, I consider quite relieving the fact that you have a past and do not try to "forget" it. Your past, like it or not, gives you some kind of support and shows your life's milestones. Once you look into your past and are conscious that all the events, good and bad made you the one you are today, and you feel gratitude, then it can be considered you passed and integrated the events, often called "the exams" you had met. Once you look at your past with bitterness and sorrow, then you are not even in the same place but that event from your past made you go back and back into your own failure. It is sad you did not learn your "lesson" since you return every time into the same place until you do learn it, until you are able to admit that things are differently seen from different angles. Once you accept that the events you are going through are helping you to grow and learn from, life becomes simpler. It is not easy, but can be done with practice.

I remember I was so stressed out I would find out, at some point, that one thing would entirely change my whole existence. And the thing that indeed changed it came as a small thing leading to another and then to another one, just like a simple link transformed into a big chain. I am not quite sure we are ever prepared for definitive changes not only because of the environment we need to adapt to but also due to our own chains and limits. If sudden and brutal, the changes might not be bearable but destructive so that we are facing the changes we are capable to integrate into our own lives, at the right time.

I felt trapped in my past for all my life and I considered this might be the only chance to get free and willing to use it the best I knew. If this new moment would lead me to one millimeter closer to finding who I was, I was willing to invest all my chances in it.

It was already my 8th flight to France and expected to be the longest one. I could not close my eyes for more than half an hour. My mind was analyzing in detail all the information I had gathered. I started begging my mind to give me a short rest but it was impossible to come to terms with it. I was so absorbed in my own thoughts that I did not hear my plane neighbor's question so I had to kindly ask her to say it again.

"What are you doing in Paris?" she repeated with a smile. She had a typical grandmotherly face and a very warm calmness that inspired you to leave all the worries behind.

"I hope to find my balance", I surprised myself answering.

"Good for you, my dear", she replied with a large smile. "Aren't we all, even if we are not conscious about that? Not all of us are so clear at such an early age. You might find it earlier as you are so young and you have all the time ahead".

"In fact I hope to find my mother and when I see her, I hope that I will finally understand why and how … I don't know. It does seem pretty complicated at this point …"

"The balance is already in you; all you have to do is believe that. The real balance is not outside, but inside you. Once you understand that, you will see things are much easier that expected. Once you understand that, piece by piece, everything goes into its own place. And once you find your balance, it is easy to see the balance in all the things around you."

"I do hope so. This is all I can hope for at this point".

"When time is right, it will come, my dear". "What about finding your mother? How did you lose her?" she asked after a moment of silence.

"It is a long story …"

"It is a long way …"

"I guess I am not quite ready to answer that, I am sorry", I replied ending the conversation. "I am still trying to figure it out for myself".

"This is ok, dear. Whenever time is right, you will be", she replied with a warm smile.

I realized that this subject with my mother being alive and not dead at my birth was not the real issue for me. My entire life I felt like a murderer of my own mother. I wished more than once, to change my place with her. She gave me not only life but also her life and this seemed so unfair. I kept wondering *"Why me? What for? What reason was for me to come into this world? Why me and not her? What is my mission? Is there any?"* It was like I was torturing myself. I was aware that maybe I was too stressed to answer all these questions and not living my own life. If it is true that the days we are living at this moment are special indeed and our dreams are coming true more quickly than in any other moment of the human history, I was blessed to get a chance to find my mother. Just a couple of months ago not to mention years, I would not even dared to think that my mother was alive. This was beyond any expectation I could have had. But then I was thinking that maybe life is giving me the chance to get more from my life and find the balance I was searching for. Finding my mother might help me get the trust myself, as a woman and maybe in the family concept. Maybe this might give me confidence to start my own family. I knew this was an expectation I might not meet but could not help myself in creating it. I was working on my shields on a daily basis because I knew that once you are disappointed or frustrated or feeling "empty" inside, you tend to cover yourself with so many shields in order to be protected against the pain. Unfortunately the same shields, created for a different purpose, do not allow you to feel the joy and happiness, also. And you soon feel nothing: no pain but no pleasure and this might be the worst thing that can happen to us as human beings.

"May I ask you something?" I suddenly asked.

"Sure", she replied.

"How did you know what you have to do in your life? I mean how did you know what to chose and when?"

"My dear, I didn't. I just took step after step. I met a man I fell in love with, we got married. We had children, our children got married in their turn and now they have children of their own. I took life as it came. Step by step. All I did was enjoying the present moment and live it. And I am happy I did. I did my best to have more happy moments than regrets and anger. Happiness leads to happiness, as much as anger attracts more anger and frustration."

Looking at this lady I understood why she looked so beautiful not only for her age but for any age. Her face radiated a life of accomplishment.

"Was it hard to do it?" I asked shyly. "I mean to find your balance", I added.

"I didn't know to do it any other way. This was the only way I took it. Just consider the times I lived in and you can understand that. I was born between the two wars, and, as a child, I experienced what war meant. I experienced the hunger, the feeling of losing your friends in a second. My mother and one sister died during the attacks. I could have died many times in the war, but I stayed alive. Why? What for? I do not know exactly the reason not even now, but deep in my heart, I think I know it. Some people survive, some people … die. It is always a balance in life. Sometimes we meet people we know will never see again and, however, we have that kind of conversation we have never had with anyone before. Or maybe this is one of the reason we have the courage to open our hearts because we know that we will never face that person again. I have had my own questions, many still unanswered, but I hope that the moment I will go up there, the place I call "home", I will find all the answers. And hopefully I will be able to say "Well, it was worth it, every tear, joy, moment of happiness and doubt, all of them. Because they all helped me to be what I am today. They were all worth it!"

Lunch came and we prepared the little trays. Between the forks and knifes, I found myself talking loud. I felt like a kid in school when called into the principle's office.

"There are things the majority seems to understand but not me and this really annoys me". "The marriage issue, for instance, seems so different for me than for all the other people. It does not mean that I feel better or worse, I am aware that I chose this road but sometimes I wish I understand. Seems like I am coming from another planet or attended a totally different school than people around me" I said trying to smile but did not really succeed.

"What do you mean? Tell me about it", she said getting a better position so that she could have lunch and look at me at the same time.

"Sometimes I ask myself why can't I just follow the same "pattern" as all the people. The majority get married and then have children. I have never followed this pattern. Looking back at my life, I knew that all the times I had to choose between starting my own family and beginning another "project", I have always chosen the other "project", whether it was business, traveling or studying. I was thinking that you need to "plant" and watch "the project" grow and protect it so that you can get the fruits from it. Since I have never planted any seeds called "marriage" or "family", I had no expectations to get any fruits. I knew I was stubbornly following another way than other people and I knew this is my way but it is impossible not to think about it from time to time. I have never liked comparing what I have with what the others have because I knew how much effort and time and patience and hopes and joy and happiness I put in my own "projects". You are the only one who knows how much you invest in your own projects and no one else does. I knew that from "outside" things might seem simple but once you get deeper "inside", into the very core of the "project", things seem to be different because they are more complex. At least this is my impression."

"And why didn't you plant the "project" called marriage?"

"I have always believed I was not prepared for it. Somehow I thought that I needed to experience the most part of the "road" only by myself and understand it so that once I join another person, we can share the gathered experiences. Since I do not understand beauty, for instance, how can I express it and share it? I found it so unfair to be with someone only not to be alone. I saw more people being alone in relations ... I do not want that for myself" I added after a few seconds.

"I have never thought about it like this. Then why don't you find a man you like and get married and have kids of your own?" she asked puzzled.

"It seems to be such a huge compromise. For me, this concept of love has different quotations. I have seen too many families destroyed by ego or frustration to follow the same "pattern". We are replacing our parents with our loved ones, we probably get married in order to have someone next to us, a "witness" to our lives, make children to have a motivation to live for and once they are having their own lives we feel abandoned, useless and empty just like our parents probably did. For me, a family means joy and sharing, support and caring, not compromises and frustration. Maybe I created a perfect world for me so that I wouldn't be able to find it. Or maybe living with no mother gave me another perspective over things. Maybe I created this "perfect world" and I am afraid to be part of it because that means that some things will always be wrong. Somehow I found it too unfair to ask someone else to "cover" all the "gaps" from my life when I have not succeeded in filling them. I often wonder which way is better to take: stay out of the circle of "getting" into a relationship that does not offer me the feeling I am looking for or stay out of it. I guess I am trapped into my own questions and being so busy with finding "the right" answer that I had no availability for another "subject". I got the feeling there are bigger things than life itself and somehow, once I'll get on the road, I will see more and more clearly where I am heading."

"You might be right here. But you must remember one thing: you can not always find answers to all your questions and you should be ready to accept this. Sometimes things happen for a reason or not; anyway they do happen and rejecting this fact, makes your life a hell. I do not say you should jump and accept everything but be aware that you do not always find the answers to all your questions. Sometimes life has no answers for all the questions. If you make an obsession out of finding a certain answer at a certain time, you might lose the time in between. And the joy that life brings in all this time," she said in one breath.

"One of the most amazing thing I discovered in my life was that mind is the one that needs answers and explanations while the heart already knows them".

"Remember that the past, no matter how burdensome it might seem, can not be changed and future is always a mystery" she added. You never know what is going to be next: the next second, the next hour. No wonder future is hard to predict. You chose your future by taking the present road. You go to the right, the future is different than if you take left or go straight. It does depend on you and you alone; it is your free will which road you'll take. Besides there are moments when you see only the first steps of the road and only after that it gets clearer and clearer. What I am trying to say is that there are cases when you have no general perspective over one road or another and this creates confusion. But once you know what you want from your life, it is easier to go with it."

"So believing in your way might be a huge help", I answered shyly.

"Definitely" she replied quickly.

"Believing in something whether it is religion, angels, saints has always made me think that it is easier as you feel you have a support you can rely on. It is like a stick you need when climbing a mountain. It helps me not to fall and climb faster and safer." I added just for myself and remembering how I was sensing my mother watching over me all the time from up there, from the sky.

"We all have our moments of doubts and weaknesses", the lady said as if I hadn't even interrupted her, "but we do not have to lose trust and faith. We can not afford to lose them and we must believe they stick to us forever. Sharing ideas and moments with people we consider special, looking at these special people's lives make us remember we are all special and unique in our own way and give us more power for fulfilling our dreams. Our real power comes out only when we ask for it. No need for struggle but special understanding in order to have access to it. It is not even hidden but needs trust and confidence in it. We all have it but not everyone uses it or asks for its access into their lives. What are the chances to have so much power and not even be aware of it? If not conscious how can you ask for it? Sharing ideas with the persons with similar interests and concerns makes you stronger. The seeds you are planting have more chances to become plants on a fertile land", she added and looked into my eyes making sure I understand what she was talking about. Then she continued.

"Out of my life experience, I realized with amazement that every time I thought I got to a so called dead end and saw no solution at all, I got out of it somehow. I learned that for every problem there are at least two solutions. Sometimes it seems impossible to find the first solution but, once found, the next ones are almost instantly coming. Comparing my life with other people caused me great pain but I learned from it. From outside, all lives seem perfect but once you get to know them, you are almost sure you are blessed to have your life not only because it usually looks easier but because you know how to deal with it. It is your life. If you have no idea how to deal with it, no one else does", she added.

"And there is also the ego!" she continued with a higher voice. "As long as you let it run your life, you will not have an easy one because it always reminds you about all your doubts, weaknesses, and failures and rather forgets about the things that are worth having your life built on. If you look inside yourself, you will discover things you are not even aware of! And they are so amazingly beautiful!" she said and put the knife on the plate.

"Thank you", I said.

"No reason to thank me for, dear".

I understood that the calm the lady had "printed" on her beautiful face was part of her life philosophy. I could not even imagine what she and my grandparents had to face during the wars. Somehow they survived even if their lives had been cut into pieces. I have heard and read many stories about the days during wars' time and I felt grateful not being born in those days. So many lives seemed wasted in those battles. So many buried dreams and hopes! It is unbelievable how fortunate you feel when comparing your life with the ones that seem less fortunate. But this is only a projection of your life onto their lives. Who can guarantee that your life is better than theirs? Who can measure the quantity of happiness everyone has into their own life? I have seen many people with no apparent reason to be happy but happier than others who apparently had everything.

I felt my eyes heavy. I fell asleep.

I woke up the moment the plane made the landing tour above Paris. Seeing this country from the sky, I felt butterflies in my stomach and a sense of strange connection with this land visited me again. I remembered that many times just listening to a French song would fill my heart with happiness. Now, knowing that I am part of this land, as my mother was too, gave me some explanation! Strangely, my past was so connected to one land, my present to another and my heart wanted to go somewhere else. It was like I was being split in three so it was no surprise I was struggling to keep my balance. I was imagining that the best solution would be to draw my energy from all the lands I was connected with but, on the other side that seemed such a strange thing to do. I was hoping that my trip here would better clarify things and make me understand. I was always kept between what it was and what will be but never really anchored into the present. And present is the only one we have, I was so conscious of it.

I got to Paris on a rainy afternoon. It was like the rain intended to take away all my worries and struggles. I let myself washed by this rain and prayed for a little bit of clensing. As planned I accommodated in a cozy hotel nearby the airport. The very next morning I was supposed to rent a car and start driving to Vernon. What to expect, what I should have expected was a huge question. I was creating different plans of approaching the situation but I knew that they will not be met. I intended to go and see the small cottage where I was supposed to find my mother and act just as any other tourist. The month and place were perfect for a holiday. All I needed to think about was finding a reason why I was getting in contact with her. I had no idea what was going to happen in the very next days and no matter how much I insisted to convince myself that everything will be all right, I felt my heart into my neck.

The new dawn found me in bed. After a good breakfast, I rented the car and started driving. The day seemed to be perfect for driving. I knew and loved so much the smell of this country! From Paris to Vernon I had around 144 miles, meaning 232 km, so that in four hours I have been there. The accommodation for the first nights was made from the States so that I would be "covered" for the beginning. Then I would see how to proceed. Traveling extensively over the last ten years gave me the security and safety over this type of decisions. I was looking at the people driving next to me and wondering what their lives were, if they were happy, what they expect from life, and other nonsense questions some people might not even bother with. I was keeping my mind busy!

The more I was approaching to the cottage, the more pressure I felt in my stomach. I felt so grateful for sleeping over in the hotel before I started this trip. The jet lag was "under control" thanks to the crystals I was always carrying with me; a tourmaline necklace has always helped me with the time difference. After checking in at a nice French villa, I decided to have a long lunch and walk around the houses. I could use this situation in order to look at the people and accommodate a little bit with the surroundings. I could have run away but I thought it obsolete (even if quite useful sometimes) to run away when facing something new.

I tried to find more information about the person I was expecting to pay a visit the very next morning. I did not find out too much: she was living in a very nice villa, across the main road; her husband had died a year ago, had no children and lived a very discreet life. She was well known as the best historian writer and people were very proud she was living there. I stopped at a small shop and bought the only book I found written by her: "The Sun King".

I came back to the hotel and started to skim through the book. No picture of the writer, no biography.

"She really likes a private life", I added just for myself.

The book captivated me very quickly. I felt like I was living during those days and "got into" one of the character's roles. At some point I must have fallen asleep with the book opened and lights switched on. For the first time over the last weeks I had no concern about the approach I was going to have the next day. I was dreaming I was part of the pages she wrote about. I was kept between the pages of the book and felt safe.

The very next morning I followed the road to her house. I already knew the address by heart and I was automatically counting the numbers of the houses. The closer I was getting to number 35 - strangely I was turning 35 in only two weeks - the faster my heart was beating. There was almost no one on the streets at that hour of the morning and started wondering how I was going to knock on the door of the house. The "I got lost" excuse might have been a good start for a city girl but started to have doubts when I looked around. Everything here seemed to be perfectly organized so that no one could get lost. The flowers were at home in this area. It seemed like they were flooding all the land, coming out of every piece of it.

I finally found the number I was looking for: 35. A wonderful white house, all surrounded by flowers. You could not know if the fence was covered by flowers or the flowers were sustaining the fence. Yes, flowers seemed to have a permanent address here. They were everywhere the eyes could see: windows, doors, lamps, alleys ... I rang the bell and waited for an answer. I was hoping no one would answer so that I had to come later with a real plan for getting myself introduced. I woke up from my dreams when the fence automatically opened. I came into the yard and then walked up the stairs to the house. The entrance door was open and exactly the moment I was wondering if I should go on or not, I heard a woman's voice from inside:

"Entrez, s'il vous plait".

I looked around to check if there was someone else next to me but it was only me. I passed through a wonderful entrance room and from there, trying to hear the sound of the lady's voice or steps. I entered a large hall. The inside was even nicer than the outside. The French windows let all the light in. The taste of the whole place was exceptionally impeccable. The curtains were all made of rainbow colored light veil so they looked like birds' wings. The smell of the flowers and especially of roses and lavender was all around. On the walls there were paintings of the Impressionists I recognized. I knew we were in their "territory" and wondered for a second if I was in a dream.

"Bonjour. Je cherche …" I started my "introduction" when I found the lady in front of a wall completely covered with books.

"Bonjour, oui, je le sais. Vous etes arrive quand?"

I had no idea if she was talking to me. I asked my angels to give me a hand when I saw the most beautiful woman I have ever seen before: blond hair, fluid pink dress, gorgeous eyes, a wonderful smile … I was speechless …

"Vous êtes bien?"

"Yes, I am. Oui …" I started, puzzled I was still able to articulate a word.

"You speak English? Great. Let's use English, I have no one to practice it with inhere. In case you do not mind" she added.

"Not at all" I replied feeling my voice getting more and more choked.

"I was expecting you later today but it is very good you arrived earlier. We have more time to adjust".

"Yes", I finally succeeded to add. I knew the very second I saw her that she was my mother. I was having in a strange, not even known way, the same type of hair arrangement, clothes color and smile. I had my father's eyes and height but physical I had so many things in common with this person I have never met before. Just breathing the same air with her was enough for me. Even though I had no idea what the next steps would be, what I would tell her, why I came here for, this first meeting was one of the most beautiful moments of my entire life.

"Have we met before? You seem rather familiar to me" she added and made me blink just like my secret was coming out earlier than expected.

"I would have remembered" I succeeded to finally say.

"Let's go into the garden. It is so beautiful outside this time of the year. When my husband was here we used to spend a lot of time out there. I was researching for my books or writing and he was reading his art magazines. You always tend to imagine the past better than it was. But we used to have very pleasant moments here". Sorry I did not even ask what your name is, bad manners …" she said with an absolutely ravishing smile. "I am Catherine, nice to meet you".

"I am Ema and I am so happy to finally meet you".

"Have you been looking for me for a long time?

"You have no idea".

"Was it so difficult to get here?"

"Oh, yes", I automatically answered. "I got a little bit lost but I found my way in the end". I imagined how stupid I might seem. It had only been two minutes since I met her and I already told my first lie.

The phone rang and I knew that my "introduction" was going to be revealed. I just wanted to run and never come back again but my feet seemed stuck to the ground.

"Seems like the person I was expecting is not coming. I am out of an assistant. Maybe it was really not meant to be." "Who are you? I thought you were my assistant …" she continued after a short break.

"I am sorry, I was trying to tell you but for some reason I did not. I am Ema O'Neill, I live in the US and I am in the area for some research for … ".

"What kind of research?"

"It's a paper I need for school, "Art and Architecture in French Villages". But since you need an assistant, I can help if you think it's ok, of course". I had no idea why I said it but I was trying to prolongue every single second of my stay there. "You can give me a trial period, if you want." I added. I had the impression that it was not even me speaking but someone else. But I was happy this person was speaking.

"Why would you want to work for me?"

"I am here, and I do not believe in coincidences".

"You don't?"

"No, I don't. It is said that once you believe in coincidences, you do not see the miracles. And I like to believe in miracles."

"I am a writer and I need an assistant to help me manage all the research part. My next book will be about Princess Marie".

"Perfect, I can help no problem. I would love to". My eyes started to giggle only thinking of the usefulness of all my studies so far. Had I taken some classes on the French history, this might have helped more; but she needed an assistant, not a historian, after all.

"OK, we can try and see how things evolve. We can work on a plan and see exactly the timing for each phase of the process", she said after a moment of reflection.

"Perfect."

"Let's get some lemonade and bring my laptop. I'll be back in a sec".

I was trying to calm my breath. My heart was racing in my chest. It was as if I had had the toughest negotiation with one of my clients. Except that now I was too emotionally involved. It is so true that once you have or you pretend to have nothing to lose, you feel more relaxed in any kind of negotiation. I was decided to use every second I could spend with my mother. I did not want to miss any other moment. I thanked my angels for being there. I knew they were behind all this turn of events. How else could I have arrived there the very day she was going to hire an assistant that got lost on the way?

"Since your mother tongue is English, you can start with the English works first, what do you think?" I heard her voice sooner than her seeing her physical presence.

"Great. However, I need to tell you, from the beginning, that English is not my mother tongue so that there is no misunderstanding."

"You have more than one mother tongue?" she asked.

"I was born in Romania and left for States when I was 14 so …".

She did not say anything for a couple of minutes. She looked like she had seen a ghost.

"Vous êtes bien?"

"No".

"Is there anything I can do to help?"

"No, no, it's ok. I'll just get some water, thank you. It is just … I am ok, I'll just get some water and I'll be fine. I am always fine", she added as if she was encouraging herself.

I was looking at her and did not understand how a person like her could have such deep wounds. Her face changed and I felt so sorry to cause her pain. I wanted to help and not to make her feel bad. I decided not to continue on the subject. I decided to take it step by step.

"Do you feel better?" I asked worried.

"I am, yes I am, thank you". "Sorry for that. My past is hunting me from time to time. Writing historian novels made me realize one thing: your past can kill you if you let it overwhelm you … "

"Unless you accept it. And let it go …"

"Exactly. Who are you?"

"I am …"

"I know your name. Sorry, the way we met is just strange. I guess someone up there has a great laugh about this entire situation" she concluded in a smile looking up to the sky.

"I know out of my own experience how past can torture you but someone told me once that all we can do is to try and change our angle of looking at the situation. Then you might see it differently. It is up to us if we take what happened as a blessing or as a curse. And we create our own future based on the way we look at our present".

I did not add a word but I remembered the lady I met on the plane.

"OK, let's work on the plan", she said and seemed to regain the grip of herself.

The plan for the next two weeks was to separately get all the information on the subject, then meet two hours per day, discuss the findings, and share information. Being in the local library reminded me of my school years when I used to hide from anyone between its walls. I loved the smell of old books. Working for and with Catherine gave me full access to all the books from that library; books so old I have never dreamed of touching. I was just like a kid in her first moments of wonder and felt my heart jumping every time a new piece of info was revealed to me. I was thinking of the many hands that touched the very same pages in the last hundred years, how many stories were written under the same pages. And again, how many tears, hopes, expectations, smiles had been born under those pages! Only if they could talk! So many words are between the covers of a book and how ironic that there is so much silence in a library!

I was so grateful for those days and grateful for every single moment that contributed to this very present. Images from my past once considered so painful and "covered" in fear till that moment, were coming into my mind and every time I was looking at them as images from me; soon I started to see myself out of "their frame", make a bow as I was in front of a person and thanked them for happening. I read somewhere that every time you remember painful situation from your past, you can help healing them by making a bow or covering the whole situation or person in light and love. I instantly felt such a relieve every time I was doing that and every time new images came over, I was doing it instantly, almost automatically. I was thinking to what the lady from the plane told me. If we can accept that everything from our past happened for a reason or not, then we see it differently. I knew I did not get everything I hoped for till that very moment, but, for the first time in my life, I started to laugh about all the plans I was doing for myself. I thanked God I was not too obsessed in getting what I "wrote on my board" and did listen to my heart. If succeeding to getting all I had asked for, I would not expect for the moments I had at this moments. And I was grateful for the first time in my life for the things that I did not get! It seemed hilarious, and only thinking about it, made me laugh. Yes, it's true: once you get everything from "your list", how can you keep going? You always add something so that you have a new dream to make true, no matter if getting to the gym more often or visiting a place you have never been before.

Being in this world, of people that lived hundred of years ago, on this exactly land, gave me a feverish feeling. I was coming from an ocean distance to reveal the life it was written they had lived. I was wondering under what circumstances the "writer" of the Court was respecting entirely the truth of the facts and how romance stories were built on true facts.

I was seeing Catherine every day for two hours in her house garden, at 6 p.m. sharp. The smell of roses and lavender seemed to be everywhere. Once the sunset was coming, I knew it was time for me to leave. It was for the first time in my life when I saw the sunset as a "threatening" point. I was grateful however for the time spent within that atmosphere and was eagerly waiting for the following day. Then I would go to the rented room and I would fall asleep but not before thanking even to the Sun for the day that just ended! I felt, again for the first time in my life, the feeling of completeness without thinking of what my life would have been with or without a certain thing. We do need so little to be happy! Or at least I found that on those moments!

I had already been under the "new job" for almost two weeks when Catherine proposed that we go to Paris for more research at the National Library. We were supposed to stay there for a week in order to get some very old pieces of work that we could not get from the local library. I was just thinking how odd and interesting would be to spend more than two hours per day with my own mother. Interesting was the definition as I did not know exactly what it meant. I had no idea what to expect, or if I had to expect anything. We were supposed to work all day long but knowing that I would breathe the same air with her gave me ecstatic moments. I felt I was in love with a person I did not know but instinctively loved. After all, she was my mother even though it was only I who knew that!

The way to Paris was uneventful. While she was driving, I was trying to find a way to start the conversation but nothing seemed good enough. I was secretly looking at her. She caught my eye twice and I felt like a schoolgirl caught copying during some decisive test. I felt so much love flowing through my veins and going straight to her. I had no idea where all this flow was coming from but I was grateful for it. Part of all this love was staying within me, too.

"Ca va?"

"Oui, ca va".

"May I ask you something?"

"Sure", she replied.

I had no idea what the question was going to be and instinctively praying for a decent one.

"How did you start writing? I have to admit that I read some interviews you gave during the past years, not too many of them, maybe I was looking in the wrong places; anyway, I did not get the answer from anywhere …"

She started laughing.

"There are only three interviews I gave in my whole life, no wonder you found "not too many". I have never had the "willingness" to get public but once my books went on the market, I had to get out once in a while and more forced than willing to."

"Is this why your picture does not appear on the covers of the books?"

"True. I write because I love writing and not because I wanted to get famous. And I will write as long as I have this need to …" she stopped.

"The need for? If I may ask …" I said after a while.

"It is like a biological need I have to answer to. I can not explain, but it became like an addiction. I have the feeling that once I stop, I will die drowned in my own memories", she said and smiled with sadness.

"How did you really start writing?" I tried to get back on the initial question.

"Well, it started as a therapy until an editor saw the notes I was making and asked me to write a book. He "forced" me by giving me an advance payment. It was like a commitment I made."

"Why history books?"

"Are you a reporter?" she asked laughingly.

"No, not yet, anyway! I am just curious" I replied hoping she will not change the topic. That was the longest non business related conversation I have ever had with her and did my best not to stop it.

"There was a time in my life when I was so trapped in my own past that I felt attracted to everything it meant past. I was also fascinated by history so the connection was handy. Writing about people who lived and died made me, in a way, better understand and cope with my past. It was like my own past was interconnected with theirs. Bringing their past into the present helped me get over my own past. It was like a "price" and "prize" at the same time. And probably, more important for me at that point, was that it made me not think of my own past. So many princes, princesses, roi et reines, they all lived great lives and did more or less for their people, but they were all mortal, too. We all die, in the end, no matter how important we are … and sooner or later, people forget about people. Writing about them is like a tribute paid to what they were and did, a sign they are not forgotten. At least for a while, until someone else remembers or writes about them again."

"Do you think you will be forgotten too?"

"We all are, chérie. We all are, sooner or later".

"Did it help?" I asked. "Heal your past", I added when she looked at me in wonder.

"I'm not quite sure but it was definitely worth trying".

She silently passed her fingers over her hair. In the light of the sun, she looked even more beautiful.

"I hope that, even though I'm not quite sure. I still remember about it but the only way you can heal your past is keep going in the present. You can make a bow in front of all the things that happened and keep going. Good or bad, keep walking, this is my philosophy".

I remembered I used the same "remedy" for my past events. We are all connected more than we realize.

"Does it hurt?" "To think about it", I continued since she did not say anything.

"God, you are really focused on that, you know?"

"Sorry. I was hoping you found a way to heal it. I have been trying for years but I got to the point of understanding that there are situations with "no cures". The only moments I am not thinking about my past is when I really DO live in the present. It does not happen all the time, though. I thought it is easier for other people. I thought that I was a "weird" case in some unclear ways".

"How much could you have hurt? You look so young ..."

"Does pain take age into consideration?"

She said nothing and neither did I. Silence surrounded us. Luckily she turned the radio on. "No, je ne regret rien" was on air. Edith Piaf, the famous singer of France, a legend for the many generations seemed to come from the past and give us a warning! I did not expect – based on the last days spent together – to see Catherine so open to discuss about things but I was grateful she did.

Once you can say that all the things from your past do not affect you anymore because they are all "paid, washed over, forgotten" and see them from a distance, in a detached way, you are considered free! I guess this is what Edith Piaf's song was trying to say. If you succeed to cut the "pain" of the past and take the best out of it, you are really lucky. If not, all the pain will stick to your feet as chains and you will not be able to walk. The more you try to walk, the heavier the chains will be and more painful the wounds. And then, at some point you will not even have the power to lift your eyes to the sky, you will see nothing else than the chains and the wounds and expect nothing else than surround yourself to them because you are part of them. I guessed in those moments many people lose their willingness to live or keep going. No matter how difficult the reality is, we tend to see it worse than it is. "Tomorrow is another day", my grandmother used to say, and things are seen differently when the sun is up, as Maria was "promising".

We got to Paris on a gorgeous sunny day. We stopped to check in the hotel and then had a quick snack. We had to get to the library and see the director. He was going to attend a conference in the US and we were supposed to meet him before his departure.

"Bonjour, Jean Pierre".

"Bonjour, Catherine" a handsome, French gentlemen answered. He was in his 60s but still looked very well. He seemed to descend from one of Catherine's books kings.

"Elle e Ema et elle m'aide avec mon livre."

"Ema, Jean Pierre Proust".

"Bonjour, Monsieur".

"You can speak English, if you want. She is coming from US so you can start "warming up" the language". We all smiled.

"Nice to meet you, Ema".

"Nice to meet you, too, Sir".

"Where did you meet this lovely person?"

"It's a long story, Jean Pierre. And you know I am not a fun of sharing details", Catherine added with a smile.

Jean Pierre started to laugh having that look of "tell me about it".

"Might be a crazy thing to say, but you both look like you are relatives. At least."

My heart jumped. I did not have the courage to look at Catherine and hoped that my body language would not "betray" me.

"Monsieur Proust", a young lady called. "Mr Smith vous appelles, excuse-moi mais c'est urgent".

"Oui, oui, j'arrive".

"Make yourself comfortable. Marcel will help you with the papers. I will be with you as soon as I speak to Mr. Smith."

"Merci, Jean Pierre".

"Toujours a pleasure, Catherine", he added with a large smile, mixing the languages in the same sentence.

"Hope to see you again, Ema".

"Merci", I added.

Jean Pierre gave us access to a couple of documents from Princess Marie's times. Due to their historical importance, it was impossible to take them with us, in the hotel so that we agreed on coming to the library every day until we read them all. We split the materials so that we get more time. At the end of the day, as usual, we were sharing the info we got during the research process and draw the conclusions. When the sun was going to bed, we were going on our own, separate ways, as usual.

Every morning, at 9.30, as agreed, we met in front of the hotel and went to the library. I was following Catherine on the small streets in silence. It was so strange to me that even though I have been in this city for so many times before, I have never seen this part of Paris. The hotel was placed in the heart of the Place de l'Opera and the library was only 15 – 20 minutes' walk away but on the small streets, behind the big boulevards; I have never imagined there was something else there. But it was. The Bibliothèque Nationale was placed "inside" these small streets that seem to be part of ... Tokyo rather than Paris. I had the impression that we were switching from a dimension to another one and expected to meet some of Catherine characters on the street. I was often distracted by the landscape but keeping an eye on her. She seemed to know every square meter of this area. The small park in front of the Library was inviting you to catch your breathe for a while and I was sure that it had its own history it wanted to share with us.

I remembered that most of the books from the old library were transported in the Bibliothèque Nationale de France, on the other side of the Seine but then I imagined Catherine working for her research in there and I found it impossible to "fit" her inside that big space. She was, in my mind, the person she preferred small places, "coated" in history. In order not to attract attention we were reading the papers inside the main sale de lecture. The oval room, built on the amphitheatre structure gave you the impression of being larger than it was. The books were ordered on the height, on more floors and, in the middle of it, desks were placed in order to get the sensation of space. The reader got all the light from the ceiling, paved in windows; I could not stop wondering how many times the sun light came into this hall from these windows. And how many readers were touched and protected by this light during all the walls. I was looking at the people reading and making notes and I could not find the "profile" of the reader as there were all ages and status.

After the first two days I had the impression of being inside the library and doing this research for years. We did not talk on the way to and from the library unless Catherine started the conversation but she rarely said a word.

The 3rd day of our stay in Paris seemed to be the most difficult one as it was my birthday. I made it a tradition to go to Paris every time I could on this day but never considered the possibility to even dream that in one year I will be with my mother on that day, in the same city. Luckily we were both focused on the research and worked until late. After saying "good night", we left for our rooms. Once I was in my hotel room, I could not do anything, no matter how much I wanted to. I got in contact by email with my dad and Maria and some of my closest friends and then tried to read something. However the city seemed to invite me to get out. I decided to take a walk. On my way out, I saw Catherine in the lobby with some people, probably her friends so I tried to get out without been seen.

Ever since my coming here, to this part of the world, I kept only the basic contact with my "other side of me" and using emails was the easiest way to do it. Speaking on the phone and hearing their voices, might have "disturbed" my strength and I simply did not need that in that period. I could hardly explain to myself why the "usual" things from my "normal" life seemed so far and distant. I was remembering them as if they were someone else's memories or seen somewhere in another life. Not only did they seem from another "history", but I felt no emotion or vibration when remembering them. My tree, the only one witnessing all my days ever since my arrival to the new house in US seemed to lose the importance it used to have. And then I felt a shiver on my spine thinking what my life would be when I'd have to go back. I decided to come back to the hotel, after a walk, and have a discussion with Catherine. Just tell her who I was and let her take the decision she wanted. I was tired of making all kind of plans and scenarios and enact them, according to her reactions. I was determined. After all, I was not 14 any more and I had to have the courage to let her know I was her daughter.

I wandered for hours but did not realize it till it was already dark. Just thinking about the phrases I would use, gave me the impulse to walk without thinking of anything else.

When I came back at the hotel, I was so tired and intrigued of my own decision that I asked for my room key and headed for the stairs. I found myself in front of Catherine's room, waiting for someone to open the door. Then I wanted to knock but then I hesitated and I felt so stupidly coward. I started to run to my own room and threw myself on my bed in tears. I could not remember to have such a profound feeling of disappointment even when my grandmother died or we left Romania. I felt it so strange to be so close to the person I wanted to be with and somehow to be so far away from her! I fell asleep almost immediately.

I woke up early in the morning with a strong headache. "Great start for my new year!" I was trying to make a joke with my own pain.

I got downstairs but I did not find Catherine. It was over 9.00 o'clock so I had a coffee and went outside looking for the sun. I felt like I was frozen. My heart was frozen. Staying in the sun light not only helped me get warm, but also made me feel better and recharged. The night before was almost forgotten and I was glad I did not knock on her door. Then, at 9.30, Catherine arrived and I was rather shocked to see her wearing sun glasses. It was the first time I saw her wear such accessory in the morning. I remembered the previous evening she was with her friends. I did not want to think of the reason "*why*" she was wearing them, but thought that she might have had her own reasons. Except the morning greetings, we had no word the whole day. I felt relieved as I could be alone with my own thoughts and focused mainly on the work. After all I was an expert at ignoring my own thoughts and focusing on work. The years of training made me so good at it!

Every time I was on a break, I was thinking at the stupidity of the whole situation and had that "what am I doing <u>in</u> my own life" feeling. The thing I was looking for was found but now I had no courage to get a closure. I was blaming myself for that but I just could not do it. I made a plan that once we arrive in Vernon, I would simply let her know and leave. That was the plan and I swore to hold it once we got there. I was looking at Catherine from time to time and seeing her so focused on her research made me feel better.

"No one knows what crosses we are all carrying", my grandmother used to say. "It's only you that knows and decide if showing it to the world".

On the last day, we finished earlier so Catherine thought we should take a walk on the boulevards and then have dinner. I must admit her request surprised me.

"Have you ever been to Paris before?"

"Four times already", I said.

"Well, I am impressed. Any other city you visited in France?"

"Provence area, three times before", I quickly replied.

"Seems like you like being in this part of the world".

"Yes, indeed."

"Any other places you have been to?"

"Most of the European cities – it's easier to say where I didn't go - , then to Asia, two times, America almost all parts …"

"You are a traveler …"

"Helps my spirits stay high, I guess".

We both started to laugh.

"Is there a place you really wanted to go and haven't got there yet?"

"There are many places I want to see: Alaska, Mongolia, Japan, …"

"Nice places", she added.

"Have you been there?"

"Alaska is still on my list, the rest is already checked", she added with a nice smile. "There are however places I would like to see again, such as Ireland, California, Chile, Brazil, Singapore …"

"Why don't you?" I asked.

"I …" she tried to answer when a gentleman recognized her and asked for an autograph.

"Thank you", he replied. "You are very beautiful, and so is your daughter", he quickly added and took a bow.

I stepped back and pretended I didn't hear anything. It was indeed painful to stay so close to her and not being able to tell her the truth. I felt I was lying to her by not telling but I knew I was too scared to tell her. I did not know how she would react and I wanted to enjoy every moment I had with her. I remembered my birthday night when I promised myself I would let her know and not be concerned about her reaction but I could not do it. I just couldn't. I preferred to suffer myself than make her suffer. I knew it was not right but for the moment I somehow knew this was the best I could do.

"At home I have two maps: one of the world and one of Europe. Each place I have been to, I marked it with a red pin; the places I would like to see, are marked with a blue one", I tried to continue the conversation.

"I used to have the same when I was … younger", she said and started to laugh.

"You are here for more than three weeks. Isn't anyone you miss at home?" she asked trying to look straight into my eyes.

"You mean my family?" I tried to get some time for finding an answer.

"I am sure you have parents and grandparents, sisters and brothers. Anyone in particular you miss?"

"There is my dad, even though he is not a talker. I have no sisters or brothers and not too many friends, I am afraid. My grandparents died so …"

"What about your mother, you do have a mother, right?" she replied with a joyful look.

"I was told she died when I was born", I replied and a shiver crossed my whole body.

Her look seemed to change quite instantly.

"I am so sorry, I did not know", she tried to apologize.

"You couldn't possible knew", "besides, it is such an old story that seems I am in …"

"Now you understand why I am not talking too much …" "I prefer to keep quiet rather than intrude on people's lives. You never know what each person hides under the appearance of a happy person."

"You are right but then you never get to know anyone and you are always alone. There are happy life stories, too, you know?" I started to raise my voice. "We are never alone but if we put so many walls around us, how can we see the sun? I am sorry, I was carried away …" I added when realizing my voice was going too fast.

She did not say anything until we got to the restaurants' area. I was not hungry anymore and felt no impulse to keep going but for some reason I did not give up. And so was she. I was like a robot following the road even though I did not know which one it was. I followed her inside the restaurant she seemed to be at home in. The waiter, a charming young man, was looking at us with a large smile. Immediately after we ordered dinner, I opened the discussion. I hoped not to intrude but desperately needed some answers. That might have been one of the only chances I could get.

"May I ask you something?" I shyly asked.

"Sure", she replied taking the dessert menu.

"Why did you agree to work with me on this project? You do not even know me."

"I do not need that", she replied looking at me.

"Of course you do not need to know too much about me but there is some basic information you should know about someone. I might be a killer, or a thief, or … even a reporter trying to intrude into your life".

She started to laugh.

"So, a reporter is worse than a criminal? The good thing about getting old is that you get to know people without asking too much" she said.

"How come? What do you know about me?"

"Seriously?"

"Yes. What can you tell about me?"

"You are a traveler, you told me that (the tone was getting more serious as she kept talking), you came to this part of the world to get a meaning for your present life (I do not know if you lost something or if you are trying to forget something or someone but you came here to get some answers; this is my opinion, I must underline that), you know what you want and you are not too worried about the material situation …"

"You mean I do not work for money?"

"I did not directly imply that but since you did not even negotiate with me the hours you are working for this project, it means either you are not here for money or that you are interested in getting something else than money …"

I felt she was reading me in a strange way. She was right: I was looking for something else than money and I came here to get something: I was looking for my mother. How can she not see what I was looking for?

"And which one do you think is the right answer?" I replied.

"There is no right or wrong answer; it is all up to you which one you choose to be right and which one to be wrong."

"So, which is the main reason you accepted me to work with you?" I asked again.

"The fact that you are not overwhelmed by my presence might be the best reason I can think of at this moment. The fact that you do not know me makes you see me the way I am. Not to mention the fact that you speak English and ... do not ask too many questions. Till now, at least", she ended in a smile.

"So you are not interested in my reasons why I'm working with you?" I replied hoping not to be forced to answer to that one but forcing her not to stop talking.

"Everyone has his own story, sad or happy. I have always respected everyone's decision to share it with me or not. It should be up to us when we want to share and not be forced to. If there is something I hate the most is intruding into someone's life", she said.

At that point, the waiter came with our dinner. The smell was so nice that we both left the conversation in the air. After dinner, we started the walk back to our hotel. There were still many questions I wanted to have answers for but the time felt inappropriate for that. Reviewing the past days and weeks, I realized that you can have the best conversations without saying anything at all. Just as all the questions find their answers in a very strange, silent way. Calm descended upon all the subjects and evening.

The very next morning, we left for Vernon by car. The research part was coming to an end and I found it difficult to get to the point I had to leave Catherine. Seeing her every single day for the past few weeks made her part of the air I was breathing.

"How is the book going? Did you get all the necessary info to start writing?"

"I think so", she replied. "I really enjoyed your help. It usually takes me months to finalize this part. In fact, research takes most of my time. I started this project 2 years ago but when my husband died I stopped it and could not get in the mood to restart it. It reminded me about him in a strange way. The day I decided to restart it, was the day you came in. I thank you for that."

"You are welcome. I am sure the book will be a success. Princess Marie will be very happy about that, wherever she is now".

"Do you believe she is watching over us now?" she asked with a smile. "Do you believe in life after death?"

"Well, I do believe that our life is not ending once we leave this life. We are going to find Heaven or Hell, depending on what we are expecting to find. I believe we are going to a place where light and love awaits us and not a place where we are punished for the things we did, do or were supposed to do" I answered.

"What do you think about God then?" she asked with the same gesture of arranging her hair.

"I do believe in a God surrounded by love and light. I do not believe in a God that punishes and blames you for what you did but more like a father figure who wants the best for His children. All He wants is for us to be happy. Because we are all God's perfect children even though we do not believe we deserve the best in the world. I have never understood how people are not able to love themselves. If I do not love and respect myself, how can someone else do that? If I do not know what I want and need, how can I ask someone else to do that? We are not able to know ourselves but we're expected to guess what others need and expect. We do not read minds and dreams. Maybe the world would be a better place if we would take care of ourselves. Once you love and honor yourself, you know what this means and you can offer the same to the other people. Since you have no idea what love is and how it makes you feel, how can you offer it to others?"

"You are right. We put a huge burden on people's shoulders. And expect them to cover all the needs we are not able to fulfill ourselves; in the name of love, we ask them to cover all our emotional gaps", Catherine added.

"Exactly. We, as people, are really stupid, sometimes. All we need to do, in all our good and difficult moments of our lives, is to see things using a filter of love and light. But instead, we are creating a painful dependency on the others. I give you this, but I expect you to give me that. This is so unfair. And once the other person does not guess what you want and expect, they get into frustration, anger, or even hate. Instead of seeing things using these glasses of love and light, they stop dreaming, all their efforts having another focus, revenge, hate or, even worse, indifference."

"Sometimes I do not know which situation is worse: to stay here, on this very existence and hate or just go to another dimension, die but love" I added after a moment of silence.

"This is a question everyone should have their own answer to", she added seriously.

"True. When my grandmother died, I was so confused and scared. It was for the first time in my life when I faced death so directly. What I found very intriguing was the fact that the world seemed to keep on going just like nothing happened. I think this was the cruelest thing I could notice. Just like she had never existed. I knew that part of her was in me and as long as I lived, I would "carry" with love the "package" she gave me but I felt it so unfair that not even a leaf "blink" when she died. Or at least I did not see it "blinked". But then I remember that before she died she told me a story according to which once the souls are ready to go, it is just a matter of time before the body or physical appearance follows the soul. And that she told me that whenever I want, I can speak to her, in our own place, created and visited only by us. She will be there, listening to me and trying, if possible, to send me some messages. She was really great, my grandmother" I ended just remembering her and being grateful for that.

"She seemed to be a special person".

"Yes, she was".

"And did you? Did you get the messages from her?"

"I did get signs. I do not know if they were from her or my angels, but I did: a feather on my shoulder, a cloud in the shape of a smiley face, a flower received from someone never met before, a song seemed to contain and "answer" to my questions. All these are signs for me and I am very grateful when I see them this way. Sometimes I meet her in my dreams and even though I do not understand them perfectly, at some point I get an answer and know that she helped me with a clue".

"How about your mother?" she asked after a while.

"How about her?" I asked back.

"Do you think she is watching over you?" she asked.

"I do not know. For years I imagined her watching over me and I was talking to her all the time" I said after a moment of silence. "It is strange, but I started having my own doubts. There are so many questions and answers that seem not to fit into the whole picture …"

"What do you mean?"

"Just think about it: beginning of the 1970, the communist regime, no grandparents from her side, never seen her grave. I was told she came from a foster home so she never met her parents …"

"That's sad …"

"If true, yes. And then, exactly a couple of days after December 1989, we left for a new life in the States. Seems like everything had been prepared months before. I had no idea that in just a couple of days I was going to leave for another continent … and another life" I added just for myself.

"Why did you leave? Especially after 1989 when the country was finally opening its borders?"

"I do not know for sure but I think it was strongly connected to my dad. I have never asked as I was afraid I would cause him pain. All my childhood I knew he was an engineer but now I doubt that very much. He might have worked for the secret services or something, who knows? It was strange, even for a kid, to find out that we can change a country for another overnight. Not to mention the fact that we were helped with all the accommodation process when we got to the States. He was expected and helped. Maybe it is only my childish spy vision, I do not know. Or maybe he just wanted to leave the country he suffered so much in. Maybe Romania reminded him about what he lost. I felt, for many years, that I was a burden to him, even though he assured me that I am his only motivation for being alive".

She silently drove through the fields of lavender and flowers. The sun was already up and smiling at us. I withdrew into my thoughts. I was thinking about my father and how much he must had suffered when he had to separate from my mother. I did not know all the parts of the "deal", but I imagined not being easy for both of them.

Looking at the fields, I readily fell asleep. I dreamed of a happy family with both my parents next to me and their smiling faces. I was a child again and felt secure and protected. It was amazingly how my inner child was coming up in their presence. The child inside me wanted to be held in her parents' arms and told she would be loved and protected forever.

The moment I woke up, we were to Giverny.

"Giverny", I said looking at the entrance sign.

"Have you been here before?" she surprisingly asked. "Except when you came to the cottage, I mean".

"I am a huge admirer of Monet's and my first trip to Paris included visiting his house from Giverny. He is my favorite painter and I consider him a pioneer of a new style in painting".

"Clearly" she agreed.

"Do you think he felt it as a pressure? I mean all the struggles and success he had?"

"I'll do some research for a future book and let you know" she said, smiling.

"You mean, you give up on princesses, princes, roi et reine?" I asked laughing.

"You never know which road leads to the next one" she said replying in the same tone of joy.

We soon arrived in front of her house. I took my suitcase from the trunk and say "good night" even though it was still early.

"A demain", she said.

"A demain", I replied.

As far as I knew, the research part was pretty much completed. The next step of the project was for Catherine to write the book. She was now in charge with all of the information; the way she was going to use it, was up to her. The last weeks were like years for me, years of so many mixed feelings. How can this be one of the best times of my life? With all the pain, joy, sadness? I remained in front of the rented room. I opened the door but only left my suitcase and went out, into the beautiful garden. I spent most of my evenings since my arrival in France under the sky of this garden. The landlord put chairs everywhere so that you could had a cup of coffee here or just look at the sunset or sunrise. I remembered the tree from the house in the States. It was quite amazing I have never called it home but only "house". Now I knew the reason why. You call it home the moment you feel home and resonate with that place. That tree represented for me more than the house itself. I looked at the sky. You can see the best sky in this part of the world: the clearest blue with no shadows or clouds. I started to believe that angels are differently located around here and not on the clouds.

The next morning, when I got to Catherine's I expected to see her inside, intensively writing on the book. Instead, the house keeper invited me to the terrace. Catherine was gardening. She was wearing a nice pink dress, in accordance with the flowers she was working on. They say that you are usually getting dressed according to the way you feel that day.

I knew that every color is carrying its own vibration energy and influence our emotion and energy levels. For me, pink reflects the energy of cleansing and caring and gives me a relaxing brightness and comfort. At that moment, I realized we were wearing exactly the same color and having, again, the same style of hair arrangement. It was not the first time, these moments seemed to be more frequent than noticed.

"Good morning, how is Princess Marie?" I asked in a smile.

"Good morning" she said smiling. "She was born yesterday".

"Glad to hear that."

"Once we came back, I started to write and could not stop till late, so that today I let her adjust with the new world", she said, smiling.

"Great, I'm happy to hear that". "These flowers are gorgeous. May I help you?"

"You are welcome, just take some of them from there and put them in this part". "I am creating a small garden for honoring her birth", she said starting to laugh.

"How very ... thoughtful of you", I replied in a laugh.

I have always enjoyed staying outdoors and working in the garden. I had a small garden ever since my childhood in every place we stayed in. Even if not mine, I was helping to a new one, here, in France. And giving a hand in my mother's garden gave me a strange and pleasant feeling of familiarity.

"Why did you quit your job in the States?" she suddenly asked.

"How do you know I quit?" I asked surprised.

"I have never met a company that can offer you a holiday for a long time and I do not imagine someone giving up on you so ..."

"In fact, the truth is that they gave up on me."

"How come?"

"With all the financial crises, they had to resize the company, reduce costs ..."

"Must have been hard ..."

"In the beginning, yes. But I knew it was just a business decision and had nothing to do with me or my abilities or qualifications. In fact, getting fired was one of the best presents I could have got under the circumstances: a present poorly packed."

"I do not get it".

"I prefer to consider myself a lucky person and not a victim. Once you feel as a victim, you start acting and are treated like one. The first thing I did when getting fired was to make a list with all the things I have always wanted to do but never had the time to do. Then, I started to get them out from my list by doing them. I realized that the simplest things brought me more happiness than buying the best pair of shoes. Shoes are still important but you need a certain type of land to walk on. Staying outdoors, reading, studying aromatherapy and gemology, biking, swimming and gardening, chatting with flowers, and children surrounded by pure nature and laughs gave me more happiness than acquiring the best client account. In moments like these you realize that the only things that really matter to our own existence are the ones usually neglected and considered non important. Had I been on the job, I could not have afforded staying here for such a long time."

"What do you intend to do when you get back?" she asked while putting a very small flower in a vase with white and pink tones.

"I am still thinking about it. Most probably I'll do what I know best. I would love working in a place with children though. And writing books for children is a hobby I hope to transform in reality one day."

"This sounds very nice", she said looking at me.

"I will decide when I get back. For the time being I take baby steps and ..." I interrupted showing what I was doing in that moment.

"Planting flowers and staying outdoors", she continued my phrase.

"Exactly", I replied.

"What was the most difficult thing you faced when leaving for your new home in the States?" she continued after a while.

I was surprised she was asking so many questions but I was happy she was not in a silent mood.

"I think the worst part was to hear so many bad things about Romania. The place I loved and lived in, the place where I had all my roots, all my friends, all my past was described in a dark light there. I remember I tried to make people see things the way I was seeing them. Romania meant not only children in orphanages, dogs on the streets, Ceausescu's death and poverty. Romania was a place where so many great things were happening and much intelligence was coming from. But I realized that people see only what they want to see. "Chance is always on the side of a mind ready to receive it" someone said. And it is true. Once you want to see the dark side of a thing and reject anything else, this is all you are going to see and get. It was the most difficult time to keep on saying I am a Romanian when everything seemed to be against it. But I did and it did not kill me", I ended with a smile.

"I also left part of my soul in Romania ..." she said.

"Sorry to hear that".

"Once I left Romania, I had to leave there the only man I truly loved and ..." she suddenly stopped.

"Did you try to get it back? Your soul, I mean", I added since she did not continue the phrase.

"It hurts so much that I tried not to thing about it. I guess I was blocked into that very moment and had no courage to continue with it. I never got the courage to get back there" she added. "Not so far, anyway", she added silently, just like she was talking to herself.

"When the perfect time will come, you probably will" I added. "Did you try to get in touch with this man?" I continued after a short moment of silence. I did not want to let the subject vanish especially now, when I was so close ... I felt my heart beating like a drum.

"I tried for years, but with no result. I had even hired a couple of detectives. It seems like he vanished overnight. Sometimes I am wondering if he existed for real or it was just in my imagination. I am wondering if this was a fantasy of mine ..."

"Catherine? There is something I need to tell you", I stopped her, surprising even myself.

She stopped cleaning the flower she had in her hand and looked straight into my eyes.

"Of course", she said leaving the gloves on a pot.

I was trying to finally tell her the reason why I was there.

"Vous êtes la plus belle femme du monde. Et vous êtes ..."

"Madam Catherine", the housekeeper interrupted. "Telephone" and she made desperate signs with her hands.

She looked straight in my soul for a second and I was looking into her eyes. I felt a lump in my throat and could not articulate a single word. I could not believe I was in this situation again, like in a bad movie, repeating over and over again the same situation.

"Madam, madam ..." the house keeper was calling.

I almost wanted to keep Catherine there, next to me and finish my sentence but I did not even one gesture to stop her. I was so close! So close to put an end to the entire untold story. She stood up and headed for the house. I closed my eyes and prayed for some help.

I was looking at her getting away and I felt like an abandoned child. However, I was glad I could catch some time to get myself together. I clearly realized that even if I had the age of an adult, I was feeling like a child. Emotionally I was a child and not an adult. I could see my wounds bleeding inside and I was praying for help.

"Jean Pierre called. He found a very rare piece of document from Princess Marie's times and her name is mentioned in it. He has just arrived from the States and can keep the document only for one day inside the library. I have to go and see it!" she happily said coming back from the house.

"This is great. Piece by piece all the information gather into a big puzzle", I added thinking about my own puzzle and feeling grateful for gathering my voice.

"When are you leaving ... to Paris?" I asked.

"Early in the morning. Since she is born, she needs to be nurtured" she added smiling.

"Earlier you were trying to tell me something" she added and kept her eyes on the plant.

"Nothing urgent. Can wait", I added wondering what was in my mind. I felt like I've been punched in the stomach.

"We finished this round. The flowers look great. You know to do this kind of stuff", she added.

"I have my own garden everywhere I go. I love flowers" I said automatically, still caught in the previous moment.

"Will you be here when I come back?" she asked getting up.

"I think so. I want to see Princess Marie growing up", I added smiling.

She started laughing.

"You can stay here and take care of the garden, if you want".

"Thank you, I'll watch over them. How long will you be away?"

"I will be back as soon as possible. Should not take more than two days" she replied.

"I think he likes you."

"Jean Pierre?" she asked in a smile.

"Oui, oui, oui", I added trying to look into her eyes. "You are blushing", I added.

"Am I?" she said. "I should be the one teasing you with this kind of things" she added while trying to align the empty pots. "I mean I have the right age for that" she added and started to laugh.

"I never thought there is a right age for this," I added laughing too.

"You know, smart and beauty is a dangerous combination", she said, laughing even more.

"I've been told that quite often", I replied using the same tone.

"Do you want to stay for dinner?" Catherine asked.

"No, thank you. See you when you are back. Have a safe trip! I will take care of the flowers, not to worry about that!"

It was the first time Catherine was inviting me for dinner at her house but I just could not stay there any longer. Not only was I not able to eat anything at that point but I also couldn't talk to her. I knew I would have been bad company. I needed to be alone for the evening.

The next day I was walking to the cottage and stopped at Catherine's house. Louise, the housekeeper, met me with a smile.

"Catherine left this for you", she said and handed me a folder. Inside I found a "thank you" note with the payment for the week and the first four chapters of the new book.

"She has never given her manuscripts to anyone before", Louise warned me and gave me an accomplice look. "She never had an assistant for such a long time, in fact", she added. "I am glad she did; she has never looked so happy in years" she continued with her French accent. It was the first time she was talking so much to me. I had no idea she spoke English.

I smiled at her and found no answer to give. I could have asked all the questions still pending on my list but I found it unfair to Catherine.

"I will read the chapters and come back tomorrow", I said.

"You can stay here, if you want", she quickly said. "I can bring you some lemonade".

I did not know if she wanted to keep me under observation but I felt rather uncomfortable knowing that I would be under her eyes. Besides, since Catherine was not at home, I preferred staying away for a while. This way I could have had some time only for myself.

"Thank you, but I prefer not to. I will just have a look at the flowers we planted and I'll see you tomorrow, Louise", I said.

On my way back to the rented apartment, I stopped on a bench outside and tried to read. I felt strange touching the pages she wrote only hours ago. I knew the book would be a smashing success; I had no doubt about that. On the other side, I was sad for not getting the "right" moment to let her know why I was there over the last weeks. Being close to her was a blessing for me but at the same time I felt such a pain that I could not tell her the truth. I have never missed my mom before because I did not know how it was like to have a mother.

Looking at the manuscript I felt so happy for her but, at the same time, started to see the gap between us getting bigger and bigger. I was divided between two totally different moods that made me stronger and weaker at the same time. I felt like I've lost my compass and the worst thing was that I had no idea where I could have looked for it. I knew there was some confusion in the middle but once I realized that my mind was playing the most important role in it, I started to calm down. The mind is twisting and interpreting over and over again all the things and events, hurting us more than we think. By allowing it run our lives, it runs the same "old story" so often and makes us re-live the same situation so many times, that it makes our lives look worse than they are. Yes, I did not get the chance to tell my mother who I am but I was very happy that I got the chance to be with her during the past weeks. She does not know who I am but it feels so great to love her no matter what. Yes, I did not grow up with a mother but that is in the past and therefore I can do nothing to change it. I will probably let her know who I am but when the time is right. I will let my heart and not my mind decide as heart knows exactly what to do and when.

I was happy I spent so much time outdoors during the holiday as I knew that fresh air heals and recharges the emotions. I looked at the sun going to sleep and gave thanks for the day.

Once I got to my room I wrote a note to Catherine and put it into the manuscript. I opened "Le petit prince" and started reading it again. This book accompanied me every day of my life in all my trips around the world. Till I met my mother this was the only connection I had had with her. For some reason, I felt it was time to give it back to the owner but had no idea how I was going to do that. After reading it, I started to check it as if I had it in my hands for the first time. I was saying, in my own way "good bye and thank you" to each page that accompanied me over the years. Suddenly I realized that the first page of the book was missing. This was really strange as I knew every single word of the book. It was really amazing I had never seen the missing page … This first page was cut exactly from the cover of the book so that it was no surprise I did not notice it before! I put the book into the manuscript folder and went to bed.

I woke up with the sun washing my face. After having breakfast in the garden, I came back to the room and started to pack my things. I was like a robot, running the program included in the system. It was still me but I was under the impression that someone else was directing my actions. I washed, cleaned and put all my crystals in the sunlight for charging. "They need to be cleaned and charged", I said. Once I finished packing all my stuff, I took a long walk in the garden and into the village. Then I decided to go to Catherine's to leave the manuscript. I did not intend to run, but, for some unknown reason, I let myself go with the flow. I did not expect to find her at home but only Louise. It was too early for her to come back!

When I entered the garden, she was in the middle of it, looking at me.

"I had no idea I would find you here", I said, visibly puzzled.

"I live here", she answered.

"It's not what I meant", I said, clumsily. "I did not expect you to come back so quickly", I added.

"Neither did I", she said and kept her eyes on my face. "Did you like it? What do you think?" she then asked almost as clumsily as me.

"About what?" I replied. I had the impression that I was disconnected from reality for a second and surprised I was still able to speak.

"The manuscript, I see you have it with you", she added and seemed to have the same reactions as I did.

"Oh, yes. Sorry, I am quite distracted". "It is brilliant; I know it is going to be a smashing success. I feel it." I said and gave it to her. She took it but did not even look at it.

"I've heard you are leaving", she said.

I probably looked very surprised as she continued.

"Small cottage ..." she added.

"Aaa", was all I could have said. "I think it's time for me to leave. I mean, you are just ... , you don't need ..." I tried to finish the sentence but realized I was hardly consistent.

At that moment I remembered I left the book inside the manuscript's folder. As I did not expect to find her home, I did not think of taking it out. The sun was slowly going to sleep but I felt its heat on my back.

"Do you have time for a tea?" she asked after a moment of silence that seemed unbelievable long.

"I think so", I added.

It was the first time we were having tea together. After our work sessions, I returned to my place and spent the "sunset" moment outside just saying "good bye" to the day. Watching the sunset is a special moment for me and I always try to make time to admire it; not only that I can clear my mind of thoughts but it gives me so much comfort and prepares my body for a nice and relaxing sleep. Sharing this moment with my mother, today, even if it was the last one, made it even more special. Ever since I started this trip, I imagined the moment I would meet her, how she would react, what she would say. At this point all these moments were just thoughts. I was happy I found her and spent special moments with her. For me, this was good enough. I did not want to turn her life upside down. I didn't care anymore whether anyone would consider me a coward or just not "normal".

We sat down to the same table where we made the plan for the book research, on the first day. Louise came with tea and biscuits. Her look seemed worried and remembered my grandparents' faces when I was only a child; I saw in their look that they knew more than they said. At this point I did not know what to expect.

"Bonsoir, Louise".

"Bonsoir, missy", she said and quickly disappeared inside the house. I felt a storm coming up or it was just my inside reflected into the outside world.

"Why are you leaving so suddenly?" Catherine asked as soon as Louise left us alone. "Why now? Is it something I did?" she added in a faded voice.

I was struggling to keep my temper. I wanted to say something but my voice was too choked and had the impression that only sounds will be able to come out instead of words. I did not even consider that my leaving was going to influence Catherine in any way. Now I understood that I owed her an explanation. Truth was the best solution but I had no idea how to start. I kindly asked for my angels' help. I remembered how many times I promised myself not to repeat the same story my parents and grandparents did. I remembered how all our lives had been affected by lying, intentionally or by omission. I really understood now that telling the truth is not an easy thing to do. Might set you free but it really tortures you first. Probably this is the reason for feeling free after all …

"I wish you could talk to me," she added and almost woke me up from my thoughts.

I had no intention of torturing her and even if I was struggling to say something, I could not articulate a word. I realized I was in an "emotional autism" situation. In moments of powerful emotional charge, I was not able to express what I felt and realized I was not a very easy presence for the people around me. I realized why I was so desperately trying to help others. It was my desperate cry for help as I felt that supporting others and being there for them, I would help myself and heal my own wounds. Somehow by helping others, I could help myself too. However there are moments, I know, when I need to directly ask for help and not wait for the other person to understand what I really need. I was hurt many times but preferred to cry inside than getting out of my shell as I did not know how and if I would be able to control my emotions. I thought that staying inside would hurt no one but myself and this was something I could deal with. I found it so untrue now because by not communicating with others you are indirectly hurting them too.

"Have you ever lied?" I asked and looked into her eyes. "Even though you knew this was the best decision you could make?" I surprised myself talking and looked into her eyes for a second. I found it so difficult to keep my eye more than a second on her face.

She looked at the ground as if she was trying to fix one of her shoe.

"I lied by not telling, if this is also considered a lie", she said.

"Lying by omission, you mean", I added.

"Yes. Yes, I did".

"Was it worth it?" I asked again and tried to look into her eyes.

"At that time I thought so. But then I started to believe it was not. My last 30 years I tried to understand all the parts of the issue but I could not find any answer. I thought about it so much that it almost drove me mad. I still do not understand a lot of things, why some things occurred the way they did and not in another way, but I have no answer …" she said.

She started to tap on the folder and suddenly, in a mechanical gesture she opened it. Her eyes filled with tears. She took "Le petit prince" and read the first page, her handwriting seemed to look like ghosts.

"Excuse me for a moment, please", she said and headed to the house.

I did not know what to do. Follow her? Wait for her out here? Was she all right? I wanted to run after her and be sure she is ok when she came back with her purse. She was trying to get something from it but seemed not to find what she was looking for. She emptied the whole containing of the purse on one of the chairs when she finally got her wallet. Her hands were shacking on the page she took from inside, well folded in four and well hidden inside an interior pocket of the wallet. Wide spread, the page seemed to fit into the same size of the book. It was a jammed, old page; however when put on the book it perfectly fitted in. I realized it was the missing page of the book.

"Where did you get this book?" she asked with her eyes in tears.

I then realized that tears were running on my face, too. I did not know what to say. I had no scenario ready for this situation.

"This is the only thing I have left from my mother", I surprised myself talking. I have not even recognized my voice …

"I have dreamed about this my whole life and now I do not know what to do", Catherine said in tears.

"A hug would be a great start", I said.

We hugged and started to dry away each others' tears.

"I can't believe this is really happening", I said. "I came here to look for you and I found myself", I said in tears. I tried to tell you ever since I came here but had no courage to. I am sorry".

"How long did you know?" she asked. "I can not believe I did not recognize you. I thought that when I saw you, I would recognize you. I could have sworn I could recognize you from a million …" she continued. "I am so sorry you had to go through all these ... I tried to find you for years but now you are here ..." ...

I kneeled and put my hands around her knees like a child never intending to let her mother go away.

"There are so many questions I want to ask you", Catherine said.

"Me too", I added. "But now we have all the time in the world" I added trying to dry my tears.

I put my head on Catherine lap and felt safe and happy. I was, at 35, a child in the arms of her mother. I will always be a child in front of my mother no matter how old I would be!

"Maman, maman, maman. It sounds so good!" I said between tears.

She held my head in her hands and kissed my forehead.

"Oui, oui", Catherine answered with tears running on her beautiful face.

"Vous êtes la plus belle femme du monde. Et vous êtes ma mère" I was finally able to say.

At last, I felt I arrived at home. I felt good and safe. The day was pretty much at the end but it came with so much love and so many hopes. My parents will always be together inside me, I knew it, even though they followed different routes of the road.

I had the strange feeling that, for the first time in my life, my past, present and future were all in that moment. And for the first time I was not afraid for my past or future but felt them all together, living in that second and not contradicted by it. By being into the present I was respecting and integrating my past and honoring my future. I had the feeling of being born for the second time in the same life and that the time of joy had come.

I know that rainy days might appear on my sky from time to time but also sunny days, joy and smiles. It was up to me to make the rain become shorter and shorter. And most of all, I kindly ask my angels to accompany me and remind me that I can fly. All I have to do is ask, push my fears and worries away, spread my wings, and go with the flow ...

Notes:

Notes:

Notes:

Notes:

Notes:

CPSIA information can be obtained at www.ICGtesting.com
Printed in the USA
LVOW102139110712

289747LV00002B/171/P